D0421932

KEEP CALM AND BAKE CAKE

A PARTY WITHOUT CAKE IS JUST A MEETING.

JULIA CHILD

KEEP CALM AND BAKE CAKE

**Andrews McMeel
Publishing, LLC**

Kansas City • Sydney • London

Andrews McMeel Publishing, LLC
an Andrews McMeel Universal company
1130 Walnut Street, Kansas City, Missouri 64106

www.andrewsmcmeel.com

14 15 16 17 18 TEN 10 9 8 7 6 5 4 3 2 1

ISBN: 978-1-4494-5104-2

Library of Congress Control Number: 2013950415

First published in Great Britain by Ebury Press, an imprint of Ebury Publishing
A Random House Group Company
Text and illustrations © Ebury Press 2013

Project editor: Roxanne Mackey
Design: Lucy Stephens
Additional recipe writing: Catherine Phipps
Production: Lucy Harrison
Thanks to Eleanor Cornford and Kate Moore for recipes on
pages 70–71 and 170–171 respectively

ATTENTION: SCHOOLS AND BUSINESSES

Andrews McMeel books are available at quantity discounts with bulk
purchase for educational, business, or sales promotional use. For information,
please e-mail the Andrews McMeel Publishing Special Sales Department:
specialsales@amuniversal.com

**THERE
IS NO LOVE
SINCERER THAN
THE LOVE OF
FOOD.**

GEORGE
BERNARD SHAW

WHERE THERE IS CAKE, THERE IS HOPE. AND THERE IS ALWAYS CAKE.

DEAN KOONTZ

CONTENTS

COMPOSED
CHOCOLATE

CHOCOLATE BROWNIES
WITH SPICED ORANGES

THESE GOOEY SQUARES ARE ENRICHED WITH MELTING CHUNKS OF
CHOCOLATE AND SERVED WITH A COOL SPICED-ORANGE COMPOTE.

MAKES 16

1 cup skinned
hazelnuts

9 tablespoons
unsalted butter

4½ ounces baking
chocolate (at least
70% cocoa solids)

1¼ cups light brown
sugar

2 eggs, beaten

a few drops of
vanilla extract

½ cup all-purpose
flour

a pinch of salt

1 teaspoon baking
powder

1. Preheat the oven to 350°F. Grease and
line a 7-inch square baking pan (see page
212), making sure the paper extends 2
inches above the rim. Spread the hazelnuts
on a baking pan and bake for 15 to 20
minutes, or until browned. Let cool, then
chop coarsely.

2. Melt the butter with 1¾ ounces of
the chocolate, broken into pieces, in a
heatproof bowl placed over a pan of barely
simmering water (see page 218). Add the
sugar, eggs, and vanilla extract to a large
bowl, then sift in the flour, salt, and baking
powder. Add the melted mixture and stir
gently to combine.

**FOR THE
SPICED ORANGE
COMPOTE**

½ cup + 2
   tablespoons
   superfine sugar

½ cinnamon stick

2 cloves

I star anise

3 oranges

TO FINISH

I tablespoon
   powdered sugar,
   for dusting

3. Roughly chop the remaining chocolate into chunks and stir into the brownie batter, along with the hazelnuts. Spoon into the prepared pan, spreading it evenly. Bake for 50 minutes, or until the cake begins to shrink from the sides of the pan and the center is springy to the touch.

4. Meanwhile, for the oranges, place the sugar in a pan with ¾ cup of water and dissolve over low heat, stirring occasionally. Add the spices and bring to a boil. Let boil for 2 minutes, then remove from the heat.

5. Working over a plate to catch the juices, remove the peel and all of the white pith from the oranges. Cut into slices just less than ¼ inch thick and place in a bowl. Add the syrup, with any orange juice, and let cool.

6. Let the cake cool in the pan for 30 minutes. Remove from the pan and cut into 16 squares. Dust with a little powdered sugar. Serve the brownies warm, with the spiced-orange compote.

THERE
ARE FOUR BASIC
FOOD GROUPS:
MILK CHOCOLATE,
DARK CHOCOLATE,
WHITE CHOCOLATE,
AND CHOCOLATE
TRUFFLES.

ANON

WHITE CHOCOLATE BROWNIES

DELICIOUSLY MOIST, LADEN WITH WHITE CHOCOLATE, AND ENCRUSTED IN A GLOSSY COAT OF SUGAR, THESE WHITE CHOCOLATE BROWNIES MAKE A DELIGHTFUL TREAT.

MAKES 20

1 pound white chocolate

5 tablespoons unsalted butter

3 eggs

¾ cup + 2 tablespoons superfine sugar

1¼ cups self-rising flour

a pinch of salt

1½ cups skinned hazelnuts, roughly chopped

1 teaspoon vanilla extract

1. Preheat the oven to 375°F. Grease and line an 8 x 11-inch baking pan (see page 212).

2. Roughly chop 14 ounces of the chocolate and set aside. Break up the remaining chocolate and add to a heatproof bowl along with the butter. Place over a pan of barely simmering water until melted (see page 218). Let cool slightly.

3. Beat the eggs and sugar together in a large bowl until smooth, then gradually beat in the melted chocolate mixture. Sift the flour and salt onto the mixture, then fold it in along with the hazelnuts, chopped chocolate, and vanilla extract.

4. Pour the batter into the prepared pan and level the surface. Bake for 30 to 35 minutes, or until risen and golden, and the center is just firm to the touch. Let cool in the pan for 30 minutes, then remove from the pan and cut into 20 squares.

CHOCOLATE BLINIS WITH HAZELNUT CARAMEL

OLD-FASHIONED DROP SCONES TAKE ON A NEW LEASE ON LIFE IN THIS DESSERT. THE COMBINATION OF MELTING CHOCOLATE, TANGY NUT CARAMEL, AND CREAMY YOGURT IS SHEER BLISS.

SERVES 6

¾ cup self-rising flour

1 ½ teaspoons unsweetened cocoa powder

½ teaspoon baking powder

1 tablespoon superfine sugar

1 egg

1 scant cup milk

2 ½ ounces milk chocolate, roughly chopped

a little oil, for cooking

1. Sift the flour, cocoa powder, and baking powder into a bowl. Stir in the sugar. Make a well in the center and stir in the egg and a little of the milk to make a thick batter. Stir in the remaining milk and the chopped chocolate to combine. Let stand while you make the sauce.

2. Preheat the broiler to medium. Chop the nuts very roughly and toast on a baking pan, turning frequently, until evenly golden. Set the toasted nuts aside. Now put the sugar in a small pan with a scant ½ cup of water and heat gently until the sugar dissolves, stirring occasionally. Bring to a boil and let boil rapidly until deep golden.

FOR THE CARAMEL

scant ½ cup skinned hazelnuts

heaping ⅓ cup superfine sugar

zest of ½ orange

3 tablespoons unsalted butter

TO SERVE

Greek-style yogurt

Immerse the base of the pan in cold water to prevent further cooking.

3. Carefully add 2 tablespoons of water—stand back because the syrup will spit. Add the toasted hazelnuts, orange zest, and butter, and reheat gently, stirring until smooth and glossy.

4. Cook the blinis in batches. Heat a little oil in a large, heavy skillet over medium heat. Add tablespoonfuls of the batter, spacing them well apart. Fry gently for 2 minutes, or until bubbles appear on the surface. Flip the blinis over with a spatula and cook until just firm. Transfer to a warmed plate.

5. Gently reheat the sauce. Transfer the blinis to serving plates, allowing three per serving, and pour a little of the sauce onto each serving. Serve immediately, with a dollop of yogurt.

VARIATIONS

USE TOASTED WALNUTS OR ALMONDS IN PLACE OF THE HAZELNUTS AND LEMON INSTEAD OF THE ORANGE ZEST.

BOURBON SALTED CARAMEL BROWNIES

THESE DENSE, CHEWY BROWNIES ARE STRICTLY FOR ADULTS ONLY, THANKS TO THE BOURBON, WHICH NOT ONLY LIFTS THE RICHNESS OF CHOCOLATE BUT ENLIVENS THE SALTED CARAMEL.

MAKES 15–18

1½ sticks unsalted butter

9 ounces baking chocolate (at least 70% cocoa solids)

1½ cups soft light brown sugar

4 large eggs

1 teaspoon vanilla extract

2 tablespoons bourbon

1¾ cups all-purpose flour

1. First make the caramel. Add the sugar to a saucepan and warm it over medium heat. Watch it carefully. When it starts to liquefy and turn brown around the edges, gently swirl the pan until the sugar has completely melted and is smoking a little.

2. Remove from the heat and pour in half the cream. The mixture will rise up, so be careful. Stir briskly until it subsides, then add the rest of the cream, the bourbon, butter, and salt. Beat to combine (you may need to return it to the heat to help it even out). Pour into a bowl, cool, then chill in the fridge for 45 minutes.

FOR THE CARAMEL

¾ cups superfine sugar

generous ⅓ cup heavy cream

2 tablespoons Bourbon

2 teaspoons unsalted butter

a pinch of sea salt

3. Preheat the oven to 350°F. Grease and line a 12 x 8-inch baking pan (see page 212). Melt the butter in a saucepan. Break the chocolate into pieces and add it to the butter. Stir over very low heat until completely melted. Remove from the heat. Stir in the sugar and then the eggs, one at a time. Add the vanilla extract, then the bourbon, and then the flour.

4. Beat the batter until thoroughly combined, thick, and glossy. Pour half the batter into the prepared pan. Dot the surface with spoonfuls of the caramel. Use a metal spatula to swirl the caramel lightly but do not overswirl or the brownies will not set properly. Add the remaining brownie batter and smooth the top.

5. Bake for 35 to 40 minutes, or until the brownies are just set. Score the brownies into squares. Leave the brownies in the pan for 30 minutes, then remove them from the pan and cut them when completely cool.

**THE
BELLY
RULES THE
MIND.**

SPANISH
PROVERB

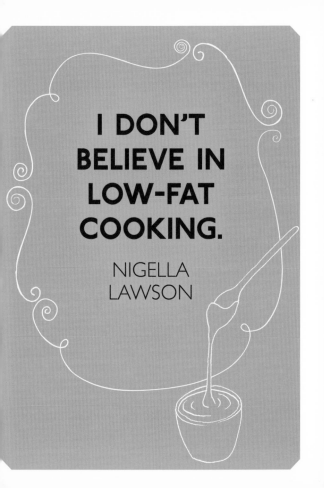

I DON'T
BELIEVE IN
LOW-FAT
COOKING.

NIGELLA
LAWSON

White Chocolate Fudge Cake

A LIGHT, ROUND SPONGE CAKE IS SPLIT AND THEN LAYERED
BACK TOGETHER WITH WHIPPED CREAM FLAVORED WITH WHITE
CHOCOLATE AND LEMON JUICE. THE ENTIRE CAKE IS THEN
SMOTHERED IN IRRESISTIBLE WHITE CHOCOLATE FUDGE FROSTING.

SERVES 12

4 eggs

½ cup + 2
tablespoons
superfine sugar

finely grated zest
of 1 lemon

1 cup all-purpose
flour

1¾ ounces white
chocolate, finely
grated

1. Preheat the oven to 350°F. Grease the
inside and line the bottom of a 7½-inch
round cake pan (see page 212).

2. Add the eggs, sugar, and lemon zest to
a large heatproof bowl placed over a pan
of barely simmering water. Beat until the
mixture has doubled in volume and is thick
enough to leave a trail on the surface when
you lift the beater away. Remove the bowl
from the pan and set aside to cool.

3. Sift the flour onto the mixture, then
sprinkle with the grated chocolate. Fold in
lightly, using a large metal spoon. Pour the

FOR THE FILLING

1¾ ounces white chocolate

⅔ cup heavy cream

1½ tablespoons lemon juice

FOR THE FROSTING

6 ounces white chocolate

9 tablespoons unsalted butter

¼ cup milk

1¾ cups powdered sugar

TO FINISH

1 tablespoon unsweetened cocoa powder or powdered sugar, for dusting

batter into the prepared pan and bake for 30 to 35 minutes, or until just firm to the touch. Remove the cake from the pan and transfer to a wire rack to cool.

4. For the filling, chop the chocolate into small pieces. Whip the cream until it just holds its shape. Stir in the chopped chocolate and lemon juice.

5. Split the sponge cake horizontally into two layers. Cover the surface of the bottom layer with the filling and stack the other layer on top. Place the cake on a serving plate.

6. For the frosting, break up the chocolate and add it to a pan with the butter and milk. Heat gently over very low heat until dissolved, then stir until smooth. Beat in the powdered sugar.

7. Allow the frosting to cool, then beat until it forms soft peaks. Spread the top and around the side of the cake with the frosting. Dust with unsweetened cocoa powder or powdered sugar to serve.

CHOCOLATE ROULADE WITH FRUIT COMPOTE

THIS CLASSIC DARK ROULADE (ROLL CAKE) IS FILLED WITH LIGHTLY SWEETENED CREAM AND GREEK-STYLE YOGURT, SCATTERED WITH SOFT FRUITS, AND SERVED IN THICK SLICES WITH SUMMER FRUIT COMPOTE.

SERVES 8–10

4½ ounces baking chocolate (at least 70% cocoa solids)

4 eggs, separated

½ cup + 2 tablespoons superfine sugar, plus extra for sprinkling

2 tablespoons unsweetened cocoa powder, sifted

1. Preheat the oven to 350°F. Line a 9 x 13-inch jelly roll pan with nonstick parchment paper (see page 213).

2. To make the roulade, break the chocolate into pieces and add it to a heatproof bowl placed over a pan of barely simmering water (see page 218). Stir until melted, then set aside to cool slightly. Beat the egg yolks and sugar in a large bowl over a pan of hot water until very thick and creamy. Beat in the cooled melted chocolate.

FOR THE FILLING

1 scant cup heavy cream

heaping ⅓ cup plain Greek-style yogurt

2 tablespoons powdered sugar

FOR THE COMPOTE

1¾ cups blackberries

¼ cup superfine sugar

1¼ cups red currants

1½ cups raspberries

2 tablespoons crème de cassis liqueur (optional)

3. Place the egg whites in a bowl and beat to stiff peaks, then fold into the chocolate mixture along with the cocoa powder. Pour the mixture into the pan, spreading it evenly into the corners. Bake for about 20 minutes, or until risen and firm to the touch.

4. Meanwhile, sprinkle a sheet of nonstick parchment paper generously with superfine sugar. Invert the roulade onto the paper and peel off the lining paper attached to the cake. Cover with a clean, damp dish towel and let cool.

5. For the compote, add the blackberries and sugar to a small pan over low heat. Cook for 5 to 8 minutes, or until just soft. Remove from the heat, add the red currants, and set aside to cool.

6. Transfer one-third of the fruit to a bowl, using a slotted spoon. Add one-third of the raspberries and set aside. Press the remaining raspberries through a strainer and stir into the fruit compote in the pan, with the liqueur (if using).

7. When the roulade is cold, whip the cream to soft peaks and fold in the Greek-style yogurt and powdered sugar. Carefully spread the cream mixture evenly over the roulade, then scatter the fruit filling on top. Roll it up from one of the narrow ends, using the parchment paper to help you. Transfer the roulade to a board and dust generously with powdered sugar.

8. To serve, spoon the compote onto individual serving plates and top with a slice of the roulade.

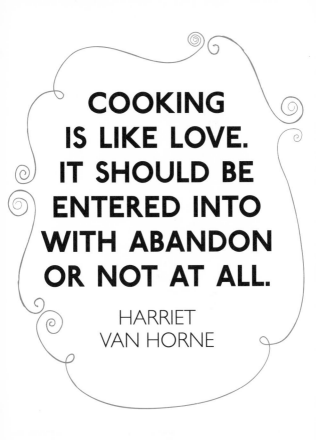

COOKING
IS LIKE LOVE.
IT SHOULD BE
ENTERED INTO
WITH ABANDON
OR NOT AT ALL.

HARRIET
VAN HORNE

DOUBLE CHOCOLATE MUFFINS

THESE DECADENT MUFFINS ARE RICHLY FLAVORED WITH MELTED CHOCOLATE. ADDITIONAL CHUNKS OF DARK AND WHITE CHOCOLATE ARE FOLDED IN BEFORE BAKING TOO. THESE GIVE MELT-IN-THE-MOUTH BITES OF PURE DELIGHT.

MAKES 12

10½ ounces baking chocolate (at least 70% cocoa solids)

4½ ounces white chocolate

3 cups self-rising flour

1 tablespoon baking powder

2 tablespoons unsweetened cocoa powder

¼ cup + 1 tablespoon light brown sugar

1 egg

1 egg yolk

1. Preheat the oven to 425°F. Line a 12-cup muffin pan with paper baking cups. Break up 6 ounces of the baking chocolate and add to a heatproof bowl placed over a pan of barely simmering water to melt (see page 218).

2. Roughly chop the remaining dark and white chocolate. Sift the flour, baking powder, and cocoa powder into a bowl and stir in the sugar.

3. In another bowl, beat together the egg, egg yolk, vanilla extract, oil, and milk. Add to the dry ingredients with the

2 teaspoons vanilla
extract

generous ⅓ cup
vegetable oil

1½ cups milk

TO FINISH

1 tablespoon
powdered sugar or
unsweetened cocoa
powder, for dusting
(optional)

chopped chocolate and stir the ingredients
together quickly until the flour is only just
incorporated—do not overmix.

4. Spoon the batter into the paper baking
cups, piling it up in the center of each cup.
Bake for 25 minutes, or until the muffins
are well risen and craggy in appearance.
Transfer to a wire rack and dust lightly
with powdered sugar or cocoa powder, if
desired. Serve warm or cold.

NOTE

UNLIKE CUPCAKES,
THE MUFFIN MIXTURE
SHOULD VIRTUALLY
FILL THE CASES
BEFORE BAKING
TO ACHIEVE THE
TRADITIONAL "TOP-
HAT" SHAPE.

Dark Chocolate Cake with Brandied Fruit

UNDERNEATH THE SWIRLED WHIPPED CREAM IS A WICKEDLY RICH CAKE. MOIST PLUMP PRUNES, WHICH HAVE BEEN STEEPED IN A BRANDY-FLAVORED SYRUP, ARE SANDWICHED BETWEEN LAYERS OF DARK CHOCOLATE SPONGE CAKE.

SERVES 8–10

2½ ounces baking chocolate (at least 70% cocoa solids)

1½ sticks unsalted butter, softened

1½ cups light brown sugar

3 eggs, beaten

scant 2½ cups all-purpose flour

1 teaspoon baking soda

2 teaspoons baking powder

⅔ cup sour cream

1. Preheat the oven to 375°F. Grease and line three 8-inch round cake pans (see page 212). Break up the chocolate into a saucepan with ¾ cup of water. Heat very gently over low heat until melted. Set aside to cool slightly.

2. Cream together the butter and sugar in a bowl until light and fluffy. Gradually beat in the eggs, a little at a time, along with a little of the flour to prevent the mixture from curdling.

3. Sift together the remaining flour, baking soda, and baking powder.

FOR THE FILLING

¾ cup pitted unsulfured prunes

I teaspoon vanilla extract

½ teaspoon cornstarch

scant ½ cup brandy

TO DECORATE

2 scant cups heavy cream

I heaping cup crème fraîche

unsweetened cocoa powder, for dusting

4. Stir the chocolate into the creamed mixture, then fold in the flour mixture and the sour cream. Divide the batter between the prepared pans and level the surfaces. Bake for 25 to 30 minutes, or until firm to touch. Remove the cakes from the pans and let cool on a wire rack.

5. For the filling, roughly chop the prunes and add to a saucepan along with a scant ½ cup of water and the vanilla extract. Bring to a boil, reduce the heat, and simmer gently for 5 minutes. Blend the cornstarch with 1 tablespoon of water, add to the pan, and cook, stirring, for 1 minute, or until thickened. Remove from the heat and add the brandy. Let cool. To decorate, whip the cream until just holding its shape, then fold in the crème fraîche.

6. Spread the prune filling onto two of the cakes, then cover with a little of the cream. Stack the three layers on a serving plate with the bare cake on top. Cover the cake with the remaining cream, swirling it attractively. Dust with cocoa powder just before serving.

NOTE

THE PRUNE FILLING, ONCE COOLED, SHOULD BE VERY MOIST, WITH JUICES STILL VISIBLE. ADD A LITTLE EXTRA BRANDY OR WATER IF IT HAS BECOME DRY.

DEVIL'S FOOD CAKE

As the name implies, this cake leads you into temptation. Moist, laden with chocolate, and lightened by the buttermilk, that sinful second helping is really almost inevitable.

SERVES 8–10

2½ cups self-rising flour

2½ tablespoons unsweetened cocoa powder

2 teaspoons vanilla extract

scant ½ cup buttermilk

2¼ sticks unsalted butter, softened

1½ cups dark brown sugar

4 large eggs

1. Preheat the oven to 350°F. Grease and line three 8-inch round cake pans (see page 212). Sift the flour into a bowl.

2. Dissolve the cocoa powder in ½ cup of freshly boiled water. Beat in the vanilla extract and the buttermilk.

3. Beat the butter and sugar together using an electric stand mixer or handheld mixer until very soft and fluffy. Beat in the eggs one at a time, alternating with tablespoons of the flour. Gently fold in the remaining flour, followed by the chocolate mixture.

FOR THE FROSTING

5 ounces baking chocolate (at least 70% cocoa solids)

1¼ sticks unsalted butter

4 cups powdered sugar

1 teaspoon vanilla extract

⅓ cup milk

4. Divide the batter between the prepared pans. Bake for 20 to 25 minutes, or until the cakes are well risen and firm to the touch. Let cool for 10 minutes, then remove from the pans and transfer to a wire rack.

5. To make the frosting, break the chocolate into pieces and add to a heatproof bowl placed over a pan of barely simmering water (see page 218). In another bowl, beat together the butter and powdered sugar, then beat in the melted chocolate in a slow drizzle. Stir in the vanilla and then the milk, a few drops at a time. Beat for several minutes until very light and fluffy and doubled in volume.

6. To assemble, stack the three cakes together with a thick layer of frosting between each layer. Evenly cover the top and around the side of the cake with the remaining frosting.

FROSTED GINGER AND WHITE CHOCOLATE CAKE

GINGERBREAD CRUMBS FORM THE BASIS OF A LIGHT PARFAIT, WHICH IS LAYERED AND TOPPED WITH A TUMBLE OF WHITE CHOCOLATE GANACHE, THEN DUSTED LIBERALLY WITH A MIXTURE OF COCOA POWDER AND POWDERED SUGAR.

SERVES 8

¼ pound ready-made gingerbread

scant 2 cups heavy cream

½ cup + 2 tablespoons superfine sugar

4 egg yolks

finely grated zest and juice of 1 orange

1. Line an 8-inch round springform pan (see page 212).

2. To make the ganache, break the chocolate into a large bowl. Bring the cream to a boil in a small pan, then pour it onto the broken chocolate. Let stand for 5 minutes. Then, using a large wire whisk, beat the mixture until smooth. Chill in the fridge until thick.

3. To make the parfait, crumble the gingerbread into a bowl using your fingers. Add ¾ cup of the cream and beat well. Chill in the fridge.

COMPOSED CHOCOLATE

FOR THE WHITE CHOCOLATE GANACHE

10½ ounces white chocolate

1¼ cups heavy cream

TO FINISH

1 tablespoon powdered sugar

1 tablespoon unsweetened cocoa powder

4. Put the sugar and ½ cup of water in a saucepan over low heat, stirring occasionally, until the sugar has dissolved. Increase the heat and boil for 2 to 3 minutes. Place the egg yolks in a large bowl and beat in the syrup in a steady stream. Continue beating until the mixture is cold and very thick.

5. Whip the remaining cream in a bowl and then fold it into the ginger mixture along with the orange zest and juice. Add the egg-yolk mixture and fold it in. Freeze the parfait mixture for 30 minutes until semi-firm. Spoon half of the parfait into the prepared pan and smooth the surface.

6. Beat the ganache lightly until smooth, then put into a pastry bag fitted with a ¼-inch plain tip. Pipe half of the ganache in a tumbling pattern onto the ginger parfait. Spoon the remaining ginger parfait over this, spreading it evenly, then pipe the remaining ganache on top.

7. Cover the pan with foil and freeze for 3 to 4 hours, or until firm.

8. About 20 minutes before serving, remove the sides of the pan, peel the paper off, and transfer the cake to a serving plate. Chill until required; dust with powdered sugar and cocoa powder to serve.

SEIZE
THE MOMENT.
REMEMBER ALL
THOSE WOMEN
ON THE *TITANIC*
WHO WAVED OFF
THE DESSERT
CART.

ERMA BOMBECK

CHOCOLATE FILIGREE CAKE

A LOVELY LAYERED CAKE FOR SPECIAL OCCASIONS.

MAKES 16

2 eggs

2 tablespoons superfine sugar

¼ cup self-rising flour

1 tablespoon unsweetened cocoa powder

1. Preheat the oven to 375°F. Grease and line a 7-inch square cake pan with a removable bottom (see page 212).

2. Put the eggs and sugar in a large heatproof bowl over a pan of hot water. Beat until doubled in volume and a trail remains on the surface when you lift the beater. Remove the bowl from the pan. Beat until cool.

3. Sift the flour and cocoa powder, then fold into the egg mixture. Pour into the prepared pan and bake for 12 to 15 minutes, or until firm to the touch. Invert onto a wire rack to cool.

4. Line the pan with fresh paper (see page 212). Split the cake horizontally and set one layer in the pan.

FOR THE FILLING

scant ½ cup milk

1 teaspoon powdered gelatin

7 ounces white chocolate

1 egg

¼ cup superfine sugar

1 teaspoon vanilla extract

9 ounces mascarpone cheese

heaping ¾ cup Greek-style yogurt

TO DECORATE

1 ounce baking chocolate (at least 70% cocoa solids)

NOTE

CHILL FOR SEVERAL HOURS OR OVERNIGHT BEFORE SERVING, TO MAKE SLICING EASIER.

5. For the filling, place the milk in a heatproof bowl, sprinkle in the gelatin, and leave for 2 to 3 minutes. Break up the white chocolate, add it to a heatproof bowl set over a pan of barely simmering water (see page 218), and let it melt very slowly.

6. Beat the egg, sugar, and vanilla extract in a bowl until foamy. Place the bowl containing the gelatin over a pan of barely simmering water until the gelatin dissolves. Cool slightly, then stir into the white chocolate. Beat into the egg mixture. Beat in the mascarpone until smooth, then fold in the yogurt.

7. Spoon half the mixture evenly onto the cake in the pan, then cover with the second layer of cake. Spread the remaining mixture on top. Tap the pan gently to level the surface.

8. Break up the baking chocolate and add it to a heatproof bowl over a pan of hot water (see page 218). When it has melted add it to a pastry bag and drizzle fine lines all over the cake. Chill (see note, left). To serve, remove from the pan and peel off the paper. Using a hot knife, cut the cake into 16 squares.

CHOCOLATE PECAN FUDGE CAKE

DARK, MOIST CHOCOLATE CAKES ARE STACKED TOGETHER WITH LAYERS OF WHIPPED CREAM, TOASTED PECANS, AND MAPLE SYRUP, THEN SWIRLED WITH CHOCOLATE FUDGE FROSTING.

SERVES 8–10

1¼ cups self-rising flour

2 tablespoons unsweetened cocoa powder

2 teaspoons baking powder

1½ sticks unsalted butter, softened

¾ cup + 2 tablespoons superfine sugar

4 eggs

2 teaspoons vanilla extract

1. Preheat the oven to 350°F. Grease the insides and line the bottoms of three 8-inch round cake pans (see page 212).

2. Sift together the flour, cocoa powder, and baking powder into a bowl. Add the butter, sugar, eggs, and vanilla extract. Beat for 2 minutes until smooth. Divide the batter between the prepared pans and level the surfaces. Bake for 25 minutes, or until risen and just firm to the touch. Remove from the oven and let cool briefly, then remove the cakes from the pans and transfer to a wire rack to finish cooling.

FOR THE FILLING

1¼ cups heavy cream

1¼ cups pecans, roughly chopped

6 tablespoons maple syrup

FOR THE FROSTING

10½ ounces baking chocolate (at least 70% cocoa solids)

3½ tablespoons unsalted butter

¼ cup milk

2¼ cups powdered sugar

3. For the filling, whip the cream until just starting to form peaks. Place one cake on a serving plate and cover with one-quarter of the cream. Scatter with half of the chopped nuts, then drizzle with half of the maple syrup. Carefully spread another one-quarter of the cream onto this, then stack the second cake on top. Cover with the remaining cream, nuts, and syrup in the same order. Stack the remaining cake on top.

4. To make the frosting, break up the chocolate and add it to a saucepan with the butter and milk. Heat gently over very low heat until the chocolate has melted, stirring frequently. Remove from the heat and beat in the powdered sugar until evenly combined. Let cool, then swirl all over the top and around the side of the cake using a metal spatula.

CHOCOLATE MARQUISE

OUTRAGEOUSLY CHOCOLATEY, THIS SOFT, SMOOTH-TEXTURED
MOUSSE IS POURED OVER A COOKIE-CRUMB CRUST, THEN CHILLED
UNTIL SET.

SERVES 8

6 ounces baking
chocolate
(at least 70%
cocoa solids)

3 tablespoons strong
black coffee

3½ tablespoons
unsalted butter

1 tablespoon whiskey

3 eggs, separated

½ cup + 2
tablespoons
superfine sugar

1. Grease the inside and line the bottom
of a 9-inch round springform pan (see page
212).

2. To make the crust, melt the butter in
a saucepan. Add the cookie crumbs to a
bowl, pour in the melted butter, and stir
to combine. Spoon the mixture into the
prepared pan and press into the bottom in
an even layer. Set aside.

3. To make the mousse topping, break
up the chocolate and place in a heatproof
bowl with the coffee, butter, and whiskey.
Place the bowl over a pan of barely
simmering water and let melt. Place the
egg yolks and sugar in a large heatproof
bowl over another pan of barely simmering

FOR THE COOKIE-CRUMB CRUST

3½ tablespoons unsalted butter

1½ cups chocolate cookie crumbs

TO DECORATE

2½ ounces white chocolate curls (optional) (see page 219)

3 tablespoons unsweetened cocoa powder, for dusting

water. Beat with an electric handheld mixer until the mixture is thick and foamy and leaves a trail on the surface when you lift the beater away.

4. Beat the egg whites in a clean bowl until soft peaks form and set aside. Fold the chocolate mixture into the beaten egg-yolk mixture, then lightly stir in one-third of the egg whites to loosen the mixture. Fold in the rest of the egg whites and pour the batter into the prepared pan. Spread evenly, then cover and chill overnight.

5. When you are ready to serve, remove the sides of the pan and peel the paper off. Carefully transfer the marquise to a serving plate and decorate with white chocolate curls, if desired. Dust generously with cocoa powder just before serving.

NOTE

IF YOU MAKE THE CRUMBS FOR THE CRUST YOURSELF, DON'T PROCESS THE COOKIES TOO FINELY OR THE CRUST WILL BE DENSE AND HARD.

DREAMY
DELIGHTS

CINNAMON CRANBERRY STREUSEL

THIS STREUSEL MOST CLOSELY RESEMBLES SHORTBREAD IN TEXTURE AND IS DELIGHTFUL CUT INTO WEDGES AND SERVED WITH COFFEE.

SERVES 12

3 sticks unsalted butter

heaping ⅓ cup superfine sugar

3 tablespoons olive oil

1 teaspoon vanilla extract

1 large egg

5½ cups all-purpose flour

1½ teaspoons baking powder

½ teaspoon salt

1 tablespoon ground cinnamon

1. First make the cranberry sauce filling. Place the cranberries in a food processor with the sugar and chop roughly. Transfer to a saucepan and add the orange juice and spice. Bring to a boil, stirring constantly. Lower the heat and simmer for 5 minutes, then set aside to cool completely.

2. To make the streusel dough, cream the butter and sugar together in a bowl until light and fluffy. Beat in the olive oil and vanilla extract. Lightly beat the egg and then beat it into the mixture.

3. Sift the flour, baking powder, salt, and cinnamon into a bowl. Gradually stir into the creamed mixture until the dough resembles a rough shortbread mixture.

FOR THE CRANBERRY SAUCE

2¼ cups fresh or frozen cranberries

scant ½ cup superfine sugar

juice of 1 orange

½ teaspoon ground pumpkin pie spice

TO DECORATE

powdered sugar

VARIATION

REPLACE THE CRANBERRIES WITH DRIED UNSULFURED PITTED APRICOTS AND THE JUICE OF 2 ORANGES. FOLLOW STEP 1 AS ABOVE, BUT SIMMER UNTIL ALL THE JUICE HAS EVAPORATED AND THE APRICOTS ARE SOFT. STIR IN ½ CUP TOASTED SLICED ALMONDS.

Bring the dough together with your hands and knead lightly into a ball. Seal in plastic wrap and chill for at least 2 hours until firm.

4. Preheat the oven to 300°F. Grease the inside and line the bottom of a 10-inch round springform pan (see page 212). Then coat the inside of the pan with flour.

5. Divide the chilled dough in half. Rewrap one half and return it to the fridge. Coarsely grate the other half into the springform pan to cover the bottom evenly.

6. Carefully spoon the cranberry sauce evenly onto the dough, leaving about ½ inch clear around the edge. Grate the remaining streusel dough evenly on top. Bake for 1¼ to 1½ hours, or until pale but firm. Dust generously with powdered sugar while still hot. Let cool, then remove the sides of the pan. Cut into wedges to serve.

CAKE IS HAPPINESS! IF YOU KNOW THE WAY OF THE CAKE, YOU KNOW THE WAY OF HAPPINESS! IF YOU HAVE A CAKE IN FRONT OF YOU, YOU SHOULD NOT LOOK ANY FURTHER FOR JOY!

C. JOYBELL C.

Christmas Morning Muffins

MOIST MUFFINS BURSTING WITH CRANBERRIES MAKE A WONDERFUL START TO THE CELEBRATIONS.

MAKES 12

1¾ cups fresh cranberries

½ cup powdered sugar, sifted

1¼ cups whole-wheat flour

1¼ cups all-purpose flour

1 tablespoon baking powder

1 teaspoon ground pumpkin pie spice

½ teaspoon salt

⅓ cup light brown sugar

1 egg

1 generous cup milk

¼ cup vegetable oil

1. Preheat the oven to 350°F. Halve the cranberries and place in a bowl with the powdered sugar. Toss gently to mix.

2. Line a 12-cup muffin pan with paper baking cups or simply grease with butter. Sift together the white and whole-wheat flour, baking powder, pumpkin pie spice, salt, and brown sugar into a large bowl. Make a well in the center.

3. Beat the egg with the milk and oil. Add them to the dry ingredients and stir until just combined, then lightly and quickly stir in the cranberries. The batter should be lumpy.

4. Fill the muffin cups two-thirds full with the batter. Bake for about 20 minutes, or until well risen and golden brown.

5. Transfer the muffin pan to a wire rack to cool slightly, then remove the muffins from the pan and serve warm.

NOTE

IF USING A GREASED (INSTEAD OF LINED) MUFFIN PAN, ON REMOVING IT FROM THE OVEN TURN IT UPSIDE DOWN ONTO A WIRE RACK AND LEAVE FOR 2 MINUTES TO ALLOW THE STEAM TO LOOSEN THE MUFFINS.

Honey and Yogurt Muffins

This muffin is light, airy, and perfect served with a little butter while still warm.

MAKES 12

1¾ cups +
  1 tablespoon all-
  purpose flour
1½ teaspoons baking
  powder
1 teaspoon baking
  soda
a pinch of salt
¼ teaspoon ground
  pumpkin pie spice
¼ teaspoon ground
  nutmeg
heaping ½ cup rolled
  oats, plus extra for
  scattering
⅓ cup light brown
  sugar
3½ tablespoons
  unsalted butter

1. Preheat the oven to 400°F. Line a 12-cup muffin pan with paper baking cups. Sift the flour, baking powder, baking soda, salt, mixed spice, and nutmeg into a bowl. Stir in the rolled oats and brown sugar.

2. Melt the butter and let cool slightly. Mix the yogurt and milk together in a bowl, then beat in the egg, melted butter, and honey. Add this to the dry ingredients and stir in quickly until only just blended; do not overmix.

1 scant cup Greek-style yogurt
½ cup milk
1 egg
¼ cup honey

3. Divide the batter equally among the baking cups. Scatter each muffin with rolled oats and bake for 17 to 20 minutes, or until well risen and just firm to the touch. Remove from the oven and leave in the pan for 5 minutes, then transfer the muffins to a wire rack. Serve warm or cold, with a little butter, if desired.

NOTE

FOR CHOCOLATE BANANA MUFFINS, OMIT THE HONEY. ADD 1 SMALL MASHED RIPE BANANA AND 4½ OUNCES MELTED BAKING CHOCOLATE TO THE MUFFIN MIXTURE AFTER THE LIQUIDS, BLENDING JUST UNTIL THE BATTER IS RIPPLED WITH COLOR.

ESPRESSO CAKES

THESE SMALL CAKES, RICHLY FLAVORED YET DELICATELY
PROPORTIONED, MAKE AN INTERESTING VARIATION ON A REGULAR
COFFEE SPONGE CAKE.

MAKES 7

3 eggs

½ cup light or dark
brown sugar

heaping ½ cup all-
purpose flour

**FOR THE MOCHA
CUSTARD**

10–15 chocolate-
coated coffee beans

3½ tablespoons
superfine sugar

2½ tablespoons
cornstarch

2 egg yolks

½ teaspoon vanilla
extract

1 scant cup milk

1. Preheat the oven to 400°F. Grease and
line the bottom of a 13 x 9-inch jelly roll
pan (see page 213) with wax or parchment
paper.

2. Put the eggs and sugar in a large
heatproof bowl over a pan of barely
simmering water and beat until the
mixture is thick enough to leave a trail on
the surface when the beater is lifted away.
Remove the bowl from the pan and beat
until cooled.

generous ⅓ cup heavy cream

2 tablespoons instant espresso granules

TO ASSEMBLE

unsweetened cocoa powder, for dusting

generous ⅓ cup heavy cream

2 teaspoons instant espresso powder

chocolate-coated coffee beans, chopped, to decorate

3. Sift the flour onto the beaten mixture, then fold it in carefully, using a large metal spoon. Pour into the prepared pan, gently easing the batter into the corners. Bake for 10 to 12 minutes, or until well risen and just firm. Invert onto a clean sheet of wax paper and peel the lining paper off.

4. To make the custard, finely chop the chocolate-coated coffee beans. Place the sugar, cornstarch, egg yolks, vanilla extract, and a little of the milk in a bowl and beat until smooth. Add the rest of the milk, the cream, and the espresso granules to a saucepan and bring to a boil. Pour this into the custard, stirring until smooth. Return to the heat and cook, stirring, for 2 to 3 minutes, or until thickened. Stir in the chopped coffee beans. Transfer to a bowl and cover the surface with a piece of wax paper to prevent a skin from forming. Let cool.

5. Using a 2½-inch round metal cookie cutter, cut out 14 disks from the cake.

6. Spoon a little custard onto half of the disks, then stack one of the remaining disks on top of each. Whip the cream until peaks are just beginning to form and spoon a little on top of each cake. Scatter with the espresso powder, decorate with chopped chocolate-coated coffee beans, and chill. When ready to serve, remove from the fridge and dust generously with cocoa powder.

NOTE

ESPRESSO COFFEE GIVES A STRONG FLAVOR. USE A MILDER COFFEE IF PREFERRED.

I READ RECIPES
THE SAME WAY
I READ SCIENCE
FICTION. I GET
TO THE END AND
SAY TO MYSELF,
"WELL, THAT'S NOT
GOING TO HAPPEN."

RITA RUDNER

ORANGE CURD AND HAZELNUT MERINGUE CAKE

THIS CAKE, WHICH COMBINES BEAUTIFULLY CHEWY, NUTTY MERINGUE WITH A SLIGHTLY SHARP ORANGE CURD, LOOKS HIGHLY IMPRESSIVE.

SERVES 6

1 cup blanched hazelnuts

4 large egg whites

1¼ cups superfine sugar

½ teaspoon white vinegar

½ teaspoon vanilla extract

1. First make the orange curd. Beat the eggs together in a heatproof bowl. Add the sugar, combine thoroughly, then add all the other ingredients. Cook over a pan of simmering water, stirring constantly, until the curd is thick enough to coat the back of the spoon. Strain immediately into a jar. Let thicken and cool before using.

2. Preheat the oven to 325°F. Grease the insides and line the bottoms of three 8-inch round cake pans with nonstick parchment paper (see page 212).

3. Toast the hazelnuts in a dry skillet until they start to turn light golden brown. Let cool completely, then grind to the consistency of fine breadcrumbs.

FOR THE ORANGE CURD

2 eggs

1 cup + 2 tablespoons superfine sugar

zest of 1 orange

3 tablespoons orange juice

2 tablespoons lime juice

3 tablespoons unsalted butter

FOR THE FILLING

1¾ cups heavy cream

1 tablespoon powdered sugar

TO FINISH

1 tablespoon powdered sugar

4. Beat the egg whites until soft peaks form, then slowly add the sugar, creating a stiff, glossy meringue. Add the vinegar and vanilla and beat one last time. Stir in the hazelnuts.

5. Divide the meringue among the cake pans and use a metal spatula to smooth the surface. Bake for 25 minutes, or until the meringue is golden brown, then remove from the oven and let cool in the pans.

6. For the filling, whisk the cream until fairly stiff, then lightly fold in the powdered sugar.

7. To assemble the cake, place one layer of meringue on a plate and spread half of the cream onto it. Go right to the edges—you want it to spill over a little. Repeat with half of the orange curd. Stack the second layer of meringue on top and use up the rest of the cream and curd in the same way. Then set the final layer on top. Dust the finished cake with powdered sugar.

CHOCOLATE MOUSSE CAKE

THE SUGAR-CRUSTED, CRACKED EXTERIOR OF THIS CAKE SOMEWHAT BELIES THE SOFT, SOUFFLÉ-TEXTURED CONSISTENCY WITHIN. DURING COOKING THE CAKE RISES DRAMATICALLY, THEN DEFLATES AS IT COOLS.

SERVES 8

8 ounces baking chocolate (at least 70% cocoa solids)

9 tablespoons unsalted butter

2 tablespoons brandy

5 eggs, separated

½ cup + 2 tablespoons superfine sugar

1 teaspoon ground cinnamon

1. Preheat the oven to 325°F. Grease the inside and line the bottom of a 9-inch round springform pan (see page 212).

2. Break up the chocolate and add it to a heatproof bowl placed over a pan of barely simmering water (see page 218). Add the butter and let everything melt. Remove from the heat, add the brandy, and stir until smooth.

3. Place the egg yolks in a bowl with a heaping ⅓ cup of the sugar. Beat until the mixture is pale and thick enough that a trail remains on the surface when the beater is lifted away. Stir in the melted chocolate mixture.

TO DECORATE

1¾ ounces baking chocolate (at least 70% cocoa solids)

1 cup strawberries, hulled

chocolate curls (see page 219)

powdered sugar, for dusting

4. In a separate bowl, beat the egg whites until stiff. Gradually beat in the remaining sugar, adding the cinnamon with the final addition of sugar. Using a large metal spoon, fold one-quarter of the egg whites into the chocolate mixture to loosen it, then carefully fold in the remainder.

5. Pour the batter into the prepared pan. Bake for 30 to 40 minutes, or until well risen and the center feels slightly spongy when gently pressed. Transfer to a wire rack to cool.

6. When completely cool, remove the sides of the pan, peel the lining paper off, and set the cake on a serving plate. For the decoration, break up the chocolate and add it to a heatproof bowl placed over a pan of simmering water (see page 218). When it has melted, dip the strawberries in the chocolate to half-coat (see page 219). Casually pile the chocolate curls and strawberries on top of the cake. Dust lightly with powdered sugar to serve.

ALMOND AND CHOCOLATE BRITTLE CAKE

Here, layers of dark and creamy white chocolate are speckled with milk chocolate chips and toasted almonds.

MAKES ABOUT 24 PIECES

rice paper, for lining the pan

¾ cup blanched almonds

7 ounces baking chocolate (at least 70% cocoa solids)

7 ounces white chocolate

finely peeled zest of 1 small orange

2 tablespoons Cointreau

1¾ ounces milk chocolate, roughly chopped

1. Line the bottom and ¼ inch up the inside of a 7-inch round cake pan with rice paper (using the same technique as you would for lining a pan with wax paper, see page 212).

2. Preheat the broiler to medium and toast the almonds on a baking pan, turning occasionally, until evenly golden, then chop into large chunks.

3. Break up the baking chocolate and add it to a heatproof bowl set over a pan of barely simmering water (see page 218). When it has melted, spread half the melted chocolate evenly over the bottom and up the lined inside of the prepared pan.

4. Melt the white chocolate in a separate bowl (as above) and let it cool. Lightly stir the orange zest into the melted white chocolate, together with the Cointreau. Stir in half of the almonds and half of the milk chocolate pieces to combine.

5. Spoon the white-chocolate mixture over the baking-chocolate base, almost reaching to the edge of the pan. Cover with the remaining melted baking chocolate. Immediately scatter with the rest of the nuts and the milk chocolate, pressing them down into the cake.

6. Leave in a cool place for at least 4 hours until set. Remove from the pan and break into chunks to serve.

MINI COFFEE CUPS

THESE DELICATE CHOCOLATE CUPS CLEVERLY CONCEAL TWO
CONTRASTING LAYERS. ONE IS SMOOTH, WHITE, AND CREAMY, THE
OTHER FUDGY AND FLAVORED WITH COFFEE AND BRANDY.

MAKES 20

6 ounces baking
  chocolate (at least
  70% cocoa solids)

FOR THE FILLING

2½ ounces white
  chocolate

3 tablespoons heavy
  cream

2½ ounces baking
  chocolate (at least
  70% cocoa solids)

2 teaspoons instant
  espresso granules

1 tablespoon brandy

TO DECORATE

1½ ounces white
  chocolate

1. Break up 4½ ounces of the baking
chocolate and add to a heatproof bowl
over a pan of barely simmering water (see
page 218) to melt. Set out 20 nonstick
1¼-inch *petit four* molds (or use 40 *petit
four* paper cups at a double thickness) on a
work surface.

2. Spoon a little chocolate into each mold
or cup. Spread evenly over the bottom and
sides using the back of a teaspoon. Turn
each one upside down on a cookie sheet
lined with wax paper. Leave in a cool place
to harden, then turn the molds the right
way up.

3. For the filling, break up the white
chocolate and add to a small saucepan

DREAMY DELIGHTS

along with the cream. Heat gently until the chocolate is melted. Remove from the heat and beat lightly. Let it cool slightly, then half-fill the molds.

4. Break up the baking chocolate and melt in another bowl (as above). Blend the espresso granules with 1 tablespoon of hot water. Add to the melted chocolate along with the brandy. Stir until smooth. Remove from the heat to cool slightly, then spoon the mixture onto the white chocolate until only the rim of the chocolate case is visible above the level of the filling.

5. Melt the remaining baking chocolate for the molds in a bowl over a pan (as above). Melt the white chocolate for decoration in a separate bowl over a pan. Place the melted chocolates in separate pastry bags.

6. Spread a little baking chocolate on one of the cups. Pipe a little white chocolate on top and immediately feather by pulling a toothpick through the two. Repeat for the remaining cups. Keep in a cool place until ready to serve.

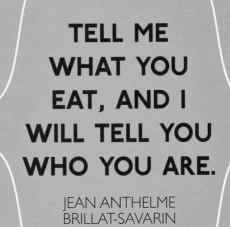

TELL ME
WHAT YOU
EAT, AND I
WILL TELL YOU
WHO YOU ARE.

JEAN ANTHELME
BRILLAT-SAVARIN

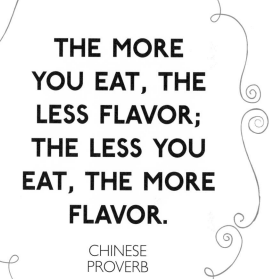

THE MORE
YOU EAT, THE
LESS FLAVOR;
THE LESS YOU
EAT, THE MORE
FLAVOR.

CHINESE
PROVERB

MARGARITA DRIZZLE CAKE

IF YOU LIKE THE SLIGHTLY FIZZY, SHARP FLAVORS OF A MARGARITA, YOU WILL LOVE THIS.

SERVES 8

1½ sticks unsalted butter

¾ cup + 2 tablespoons superfine sugar

zest of 2 limes

3 eggs

1¼ cups self-rising flour

juice of 1 lime

1 tablespoon tequila

1 teaspoon Triple Sec

FOR THE SYRUP

½ cup superfine sugar

zest and juice of 2 limes

1 tablespoon tequila

1 teaspoon Triple Sec

1. Preheat the oven to 350°F. Grease the inside and line the bottom of a deep, round 8-inch cake pan with a removable bottom (see page 212).

2. Beat together the butter, superfine sugar, and lime zest with an electric mixer until very light and fluffy. Beat in the eggs one at a time, alternating with tablespoons of flour, then lightly fold in the rest of the flour.

3. Stir in the lime juice, tequila, and Triple Sec, then pour the batter into the prepared cake pan. Bake for 30 to 35 minutes, or until well risen, firm, and golden brown.

TO DECORATE

a few very thin, long
    curls of lime zest
a pinch of sea salt
    (optional)

4. Make the syrup. Gently heat the superfine sugar in a saucepan with the lime juice and zest. When the sugar has dissolved, leave on very low heat for 3 minutes, then add the tequila and Triple Sec. Cook for another minute, then strain into a pitcher.

5. While the cake is still hot, pierce it all over the top surface with a skewer. Pour the syrup over the top of the cake, letting it trickle down into the holes. The syrup will make the cake fragile, so let it cool completely before removing the sides of the pan and transferring the cake to a serving plate. Decorate with strips of lime zest and some crumbled sea salt, if desired.

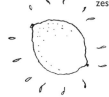

LEMON CURD AND BLUEBERRY CUPCAKES

THESE CUPCAKES CONCEAL TWO SURPRISES—JUICY BAKED
BLUEBERRIES AND A LEMON CURD CENTER. THE TART BLUEBERRIES
PERFECTLY BALANCE OUT THE BUTTERY LEMON CURD.

MAKES 12

7 tablespoons salted
  butter, softened
½ cup superfine sugar
2 eggs, lightly beaten
finely grated zest
  of 1 lemon
¾ cup self-rising flour
1 scant cup
  blueberries

1. Preheat the oven to 350°F. Line a 12-
cup muffin pan with paper baking cups.

2. Cream the butter and sugar in a large
bowl until light and fluffy. Stir in the lightly
beaten eggs, then add the lemon zest. Sift
the flour onto the mixture and then fold
it in.

3. Spoon a tablespoon of batter into
each paper baking cup, followed by a few
blueberries. Smooth the batter over the
top to cover the blueberries. Bake for 12
to 14 minutes, or until the cakes are light
golden brown and spring back when you
touch them. Remove from the oven and
let cool.

FOR THE TOPPING

3 tablespoons lemon curd

juice of ½ lemon

2¼ cups powdered sugar

TO DECORATE

12 blueberries

4. Put the lemon curd into a pastry bag with a fine tip and insert the end of the tip into the center of a cupcake. Squeeze firmly for a second to inject some lemon curd in the cupcake, then carefully withdraw the tip. Repeat with the remaining cupcakes. Set aside.

5. To make the frosting, mix the lemon juice with the powdered sugar to make a thick but spreadable consistency. Spread frosting onto each cupcake, then immediately pipe a swirl of lemon curd onto the frosting before it sets. Decorate each one with a blueberry.

Note

THESE CUPCAKES CONTAIN FRESH FRUIT AND WILL NOT KEEP FOR MORE THAN A COUPLE OF DAYS.

HAZELNUT AND CHOCOLATE MERINGUE CAKE

Two layers of subtly spiced meringue, laced with two-tone chocolate pieces, provide a delicious contrast to the lightly whipped cream and hazelnut praline.

SERVES 10

1 cup skinned hazelnuts

5 egg whites

1¼ cups superfine sugar

½ teaspoon ground pumpkin pie spice

2½ ounces white chocolate, chopped

2½ ounces baking chocolate (at least 70% cocoa solids), chopped

1. Line two cookie sheets with nonstick parchment paper. Draw a 9-inch circle on one sheet, using a plate as a guide. On the other sheet, draw a 7-inch circle. Turn the paper over. Preheat the oven to 275°F.

2. To make the meringue, lightly toast the hazelnuts in a dry skillet over medium heat, then chop roughly. Beat the egg whites in a bowl until stiff. Slowly beat in the sugar, a tablespoon at a time, beating well between each addition until the meringue is stiff and very shiny. Beat in the spice with the last of the sugar. Carefully fold in the chopped hazelnuts and the white and baking chocolate.

½ cup skinned
  hazelnuts

½ cup + 2
  tablespoons
  superfine sugar

1¼ cups heavy cream

1 tablespoon
  unsweetened cocoa
  powder, for dusting

3. Spoon the meringue onto the circles, then spread neatly into disks. Bake for about 1½ hours, or until dry and the undersides are firm when tapped. Turn off the oven but leave the meringues inside to cool.

4. For the praline, lightly oil a baking pan. Put the hazelnuts in a small heavy pan with the sugar. Place over low heat, stirring until the sugar melts. Continue cooking until the mixture caramelizes to a rich golden-brown color, then pour onto the baking pan. Let the mixture cool and harden.

5. Place the praline in a sturdy plastic bag and beat with a rolling pin until very coarsely crushed.

6. Carefully transfer the larger meringue to a serving plate. Whip the cream until soft peaks form, then spread it all onto the meringue. Scatter with the crushed praline then stack the smaller meringue on top. Dust the surface with cocoa powder to serve.

FRUITY
FAVORITES

HOLLY CHRISTMAS CAKE

THIS SIMPLE, ELEGANT CHRISTMAS CAKE IS TOPPED WITH PEAKED ROYAL ICING.

SERVES 12–14

heaping ¼ cup candied red cherries, roughly chopped

2¾ cups raisins

1¼ cups currants

1¼ cups golden raisins

¾ cup chopped mixed candied peel

3 tablespoons brandy

1½ sticks unsalted butter

1 cup dark brown sugar

3 eggs

1¾ cups all-purpose flour

1 tablespoon dark molasses

1. Preheat the oven to 275°F. Grease the inside and line the bottom of a deep 8-inch round cake pan (see page 212). Place the candied cherries, raisins, currants, golden raisins, candied peel, and brandy in a bowl. Stir to combine.

2. In a separate bowl, cream the butter and sugar together until light and fluffy. Slowly beat in the eggs, adding a little of the flour to stop the mixture from curdling. Beat in the molasses. Sift the remaining flour and spices onto the mixture and then fold them in. Gently stir in the fruit mixture and the nuts.

3. Pour the batter into the prepared pan and level the surface. Bake for 3¼ to 3¾ hours, or until a skewer inserted in the

1 teaspoon each
ground pumpkin pie
spice, nutmeg, and
cinnamon

½ cup Brazil nuts,
roughly chopped

½ cup walnuts,
roughly chopped

TO FINISH

3 tablespoons apricot
jam

1½ pounds marzipan

3 egg whites

1 tablespoon glycerin

1½ pounds powdered
sugar

center comes out clean. Let cool, then remove the cake from the pan and wrap it in a double thickness of foil. The cake can now be stored in a cool, dry place for up to 2 months.

4. To finish the cake, heat the apricot jam until melted, then press through a sieve into a bowl and stir in 1 tablespoon of hot water. Brush the cake with the apricot glaze and then cover with marzipan (see page 217).

5. To make the royal icing, mix the egg whites, glycerin, and a little of the powdered sugar in a bowl. Slowly beat in the remaining powdered sugar until the royal icing is stiff and stands up in soft peaks.

6. Use a generous half of the icing to cover around the side of the cake, spreading it evenly with a metal spatula. Trim off any excess royal icing around the top. Let dry for 24 hours.

7. Spread the remaining royal icing all over the top of the cake. Use a metal spatula to pull up peaks, letting some overhang the side of the cake.

THE WORST GIFT IS FRUITCAKE. THERE IS ONLY ONE FRUITCAKE IN THE ENTIRE WORLD, AND PEOPLE KEEP SENDING IT TO EACH OTHER.

JOHNNY CARSON

HUMMINGBIRD CAKE

THIS FAMOUS CAKE HAILS FROM THE DEEP SOUTH. THE BANANAS
AND PINEAPPLE MAKE IT FABULOUSLY MOIST.

SERVES 8–10

2 cups all-purpose flour

I teaspoon baking soda

½ cup + 2 tablespoons superfine sugar

¾ cup light brown sugar

3 large eggs

¾ cup sunflower oil

I teaspoon vanilla extract

½ cup walnuts, finely chopped

3 large bananas, mashed

¾ cup canned pineapple, drained and diced

1. Preheat the oven to 350°F. Grease the insides and line the bottoms of two deep 8-inch round cake pans (see page 212). Sift together the flour and the baking soda into a bowl and set aside.

2. In a food processor, beat together the sugars and eggs. Then, with the motor still running, gradually add all the oil and the vanilla extract. Fold in the flour mixture, a little at a time, then add the walnuts, bananas, and pineapple.

3. Divide the batter between the prepared pans. Bake for 30 to 35 minutes, or until well risen and firm to the touch. Remove from the oven and let cool in the pans.

FOR THE CREAM-CHEESE FROSTING

1¼ cups cream cheese

5 tablespoons unsalted butter, softened

1 teaspoon orange-flower water (optional)

1 tablespoon orange juice

1 pound powdered sugar

TO DECORATE

½ cup very finely chopped walnuts

4. To make the frosting, beat together the cream cheese, butter, orange-flower water, if using, and the orange juice until soft. Gradually sift in the powdered sugar, folding in until well combined. Beat until the frosting has increased dramatically in volume and is very fluffy. This should take approximately 5 minutes.

5. To assemble, remove the cakes from the pans. Set one of the cakes on a serving plate and spread the top with some of the frosting. Stack the other cake on top. Cover the top and around the side of the cake with frosting, using a metal spatula to make it smooth.

6. Decorate with the finely chopped walnuts. There are various ways to do this. You can scatter the top and/or around the side of the cake with the walnuts to cover. Or cut out a stencil from a piece of thin cardboard in the shape of a hummingbird. Set the stencil on the cake, fill it in with finely ground walnuts, and then carefully lift the stencil off of the cake for a really stunning effect.

CELEBRATION CAKE

LUSTER POWDER AND FRESH FLOWERS MAKE THIS CAKE THE PERFECT
CENTERPIECE FOR AN ANNIVERSARY, WEDDING, OR BIRTHDAY PARTY.

SERVES 40

1¼ cups candied red
cherries

3¼ pounds mixed
dried fruit

1¾ cups chopped
mixed candied peel

zest of 1 orange

¼ cup Cointreau

3¼ sticks unsalted
butter, softened

2½ cups dark
brown sugar

5 eggs

3¾ cups all-purpose
flour

1. Quarter the candied cherries and
place in a large bowl with the dried fruit,
candied peel, and orange zest. Add the
Cointreau, stir lightly, cover, and let soak
for several hours or overnight.

2. Grease the inside and line the bottom
of a deep 10-inch round cake pan (see
page 212).

3. Preheat the oven to 275°F. Cream the
butter and sugar together in a bowl until
light and fluffy. Beat in the eggs, one at a
time, adding a little of the flour with each
egg to stop the mixture from curdling. Sift
the remaining flour onto the mixture, then
fold to combine. Add the soaked fruits and
stir until evenly mixed.

TO DECORATE

3 tablespoons apricot jam

2 pounds marzipan

ivory food coloring

2 pounds ready-to-roll gum paste

pearl luster dusting powder

toothpick

selection of fresh flowers, such as gerberas and roses

4. Add the batter to the prepared pan and bake for 3½ to 4 hours, or until a skewer inserted in the center comes out clean. Let cool in the pan. When cool, remove the cake from the pan and wrap in a double thickness of foil. The cake can now be stored in a cool, dry place for up to 2 months.

5. To decorate the cake, warm the apricot jam and press through a sieve into a bowl. Stir in 1 tablespoon of hot water. Brush the cake all over with the apricot glaze and cover with the marzipan (see page 217).

6. Knead a little ivory food coloring into the gum paste. Use the gum paste to cover the cake (see page 218). Roll 40 small balls from the gum paste trimmings, the same size as a small bead. Leave to harden overnight.

7. The next day, once the gum paste balls have hardened, moisten a little pearl dusting powder with water. Roll the gum paste balls in the powder to give them a subtle sheen.

8. Dip the end of a toothpick in a little water and use it to create random indentations in the side of the cake. Gently press the gum paste balls into the indentations to create any kind of pattern you like.

9. Just before serving, arrange fresh flowers on top of the cake for a special festive finish.

THE MOST
DANGEROUS
FOOD IS
WEDDING
CAKE.

JAMES
THURBER

CINNAMON AND APPLE CRUMB CAKE

THE FLAVORS OF APPLE AND CINNAMON ARE A MATCH MADE IN HEAVEN. THIS CAKE HAS A CRUMB TOPPING THAT ADDS A DELICIOUS CRUNCH TO THE MOIST, SPICY SPONGE CAKE.

SERVES 8

2 cups self-rising flour

1 teaspoon ground cinnamon

¼ teaspoon ground cloves

¼ teaspoon ground nutmeg

1¼ sticks unsalted butter, softened

1 cup light brown sugar

2 large eggs

scant ½ cup milk

2 apples, peeled, cored, and sliced into half-moons

1. Preheat the oven to 350°F. Grease the inside and line the bottom of a deep 8-inch round cake pan with a removable bottom (see page 212).

2. Sift together the flour and spices. Beat the butter until soft in the bowl of an electric stand mixer, then add the sugar. Continue to beat together until very light and fluffy. Add the eggs, one by one, alternating with a tablespoon of the flour and spice mixture to prevent it from curdling.

FOR THE CRUMB TOPPING

scant ¾ cup self-rising flour

½ teaspoon ground cinnamon

a pinch of ground cloves

a pinch of ground nutmeg

½ cup Demerara sugar (or ¼ cup + 1 tablespoon light brown sugar)

2 tablespoons unsalted butter

½ cup finely chopped pecans

TO SERVE

crème fraîche or sour cream

3. Fold in the rest of the flour and spices, then pour in the milk. Stir until you have a fairly firm dropping consistency. Pour the batter into the prepared pan and arrange the apple slices on top.

4. Make the crumb topping by mixing together the flour, spices, and sugar in a bowl. Cut the butter into the mixture, then stir in the pecans. Scatter the topping over the apples.

5. Bake for about an hour, or until the cake is firm to the touch and a skewer inserted in the center comes out clean. Let the cake cool in the pan for 30 minutes, then transfer it to a serving plate. This cake is delicious served with crème fraîche or sour cream.

ALMOND AND APRICOT ROULADE

FRESH, RIPE APRICOTS AND CRÈME FRAÎCHE ARE ENCASED INSIDE AN ALMOND ROULADE AND DRIZZLED WITH AMARETTO.

SERVES 8

¼ cup sliced almonds

5 eggs, separated

¾ cup superfine sugar

1 teaspoon vanilla extract

½ cup marzipan, grated

3 tablespoons all-purpose flour

1. Preheat the oven to 350°F. Grease and line the bottom of a 13 x 9-inch jelly roll pan with nonstick parchment paper (see page 213). Scatter the paper evenly with the sliced almonds.

2. Whisk the egg yolks with ½ cup of the sugar until fluffy. Stir in the vanilla extract and grated marzipan. Sift the flour onto the mixture, then fold it in.

3. In another bowl, beat the egg whites until stiff. Gradually beat in the remaining sugar. Using a large metal spoon, carefully fold one-quarter of the egg whites into the marzipan mixture to loosen it, then fold in the remainder.

FOR THE FILLING

superfine sugar,
  for dusting

3 tablespoons
  amaretto

6 ripe apricots

1¼ cups crème
  fraîche or sour
  cream

TO FINISH

superfine sugar,
  for dusting

4. Pour the batter into the prepared pan, gently easing it into the corners. Bake for about 20 minutes, or until well risen and just firm to the touch. Remove from the oven and cover with a sheet of nonstick parchment paper and a damp dish towel. Let cool.

5. Remove the towel and invert the roulade (and paper) onto a cookie sheet. Peel off the lining paper. Sprinkle another piece of nonstick parchment paper with superfine sugar and flip the roulade onto it. Drizzle all over with the amaretto.

6. Halve and pit the apricots, then cut the fruit into small pieces. Spread the crème fraîche or sour cream evenly all over the roulade and scatter with the apricots. Starting at one of the narrow ends, roll up the roulade, using the parchment paper to help you. Transfer to a serving plate and dust with superfine sugar to serve.

CRUMBLY APPLE AND CHEESE CAKE

THIS MOIST, CRUMBLY FRUITCAKE CONCEALS A LAYER OF TART CAERPHILLY CHEESE, WHICH PERFECTLY COMPLEMENTS THE SWEET TANGY FLAVOR OF THE APPLES.

SERVES 10

1¼ cups self-rising flour

1 teaspoon baking powder

½ cup light brown sugar

heaping ¼ cup raisins

heaping ¼ cup golden raisins

½ cup Brazil nuts, roughly chopped

1¼ pounds apples, peeled, cored, and thinly sliced

2 eggs

1. Preheat the oven to 350°F. Grease the bottom of a 2-inch-deep, 9½-inch round pan with a removable bottom (see page 212).

2. Sift the flour and baking powder into a bowl. Stir in the sugar, raisins, golden raisins, nuts, and apples, and combine evenly. Beat the eggs with the oil and add to the dry ingredients. Stir until the flour mixture is moistened and everything is evenly incorporated.

scant ½ cup
  sunflower oil
8 ounces Caerphilly
  cheese, crumbled

TO FINISH
1 tablespoon
  powdered sugar,
  for dusting

3. Add half of the batter to the prepared pan and level it with a metal spatula. Scatter evenly with the crumbled cheese, then cover with the remaining batter. Spread the batter to the edges of the pan but do not smooth the top (see note).

4. Bake for 50 minutes to 1 hour, or until golden and just firm. Let cool in the pan for 10 minutes, then transfer the cake to a wire rack. Serve warm, dusted with powdered sugar.

NOTE

DO NOT SMOOTH THE SECOND LAYER OF CAKE MIXTURE TOO NEATLY; A ROUGH SURFACE GIVES A MORE INTERESTING FINISH.

FRUITCAKE WITH CANDIED FRUITS

AN IMPRESSIVE ARRANGEMENT OF COLORFUL CANDIED FRUITS PERFECTLY OFFSETS THIS CRUMBLY AND EXCEPTIONALLY MOIST FRUITCAKE.

SERVES 12

3¼ cups dried apple rings

3¼ cups mixed dried fruit

1 cup dark brown sugar

1½ sticks unsalted butter

1 generous cup cold black tea

2¾ cups self-rising flour

1 teaspoon baking powder

1 tablespoon ground pumpkin pie spice

1 egg

1. Preheat the oven to 325°F. Grease the inside and line the bottom of a deep 9-inch round cake pan (see page 212).

2. Roughly chop the apples and place in a saucepan with the mixed dried fruit, sugar, butter, and tea. Bring to a boil, reduce the heat, and simmer gently for 5 minutes. Remove from the heat and let cool completely.

3. Sift the flour, baking powder, and mixed spice into a large bowl. Add the cooled fruit mixture, egg, molasses, ginger, and liquid. Beat well until the ingredients are evenly combined.

2 tablespoons dark molasses

3½ ounces candied ginger pieces

TO DECORATE

¼ cup apricot jam

1 pound mixed candied fruits (pears, plums, cherries, pineapple, etc.)

4. Pour the batter into the prepared pan and level the surface with a metal spatula. Bake for 1 to 1¼ hours, or until a skewer inserted in the center of the cake comes out clean. Leave in the pan for 15 minutes, then invert the cake onto a wire rack to cool.

5. To finish the cake, heat the apricot jam in a small saucepan until softened, then press through a sieve into a bowl. Brush a little of the warm apricot glaze over the cake.

6. Cut any larger pieces of candied fruit into small wedges or slices. Arrange the fruit on the cake, then brush with the remaining glaze.

VARIATIONS

FOR A MORE EVERYDAY FRUITCAKE, OMIT THE CANDIED FRUIT TOPPING. INSTEAD, DUST THE TOP OF THE CAKE GENEROUSLY WITH DARK BROWN SUGAR OR DECORATE WITH WHOLE BLANCHED ALMONDS BEFORE BAKING.

STRAWBERRY SHORTCAKE WITH ROSE CHANTILLY CREAM

NOT QUITE A PASTRY, NOT QUITE A SPONGE CAKE, IT'S A SINGLE LAYER PILED HIGH WITH CREAM, STRAWBERRIES, AND ROSE PETALS.

SERVES 8

¾ cup ground almonds

2 sticks unsalted butter

½ cup superfine sugar

1 egg yolk

½ teaspoon rose water

2½ cups all-purpose flour

1 teaspoon baking powder

1. Preheat the oven to 300°F. Grease the bottom of a 9½-inch round cake pan with a removable bottom, then dust it with flour (see page 213). Sprinkle a tablespoon of the ground almonds evenly in the bottom.

2. Beat the butter and sugar together until light and fluffy. Beat in the egg and the rose water, then add the flour, baking powder, and the remaining ground almonds. You will have a very soft dough, which you can just about form into a ball.

FOR THE TOPPING

1 scant cup heavy cream

2 tablespoons powdered sugar, separated

a few drops of rose water

2½ cups strawberries

1 teaspoon lemon juice

TO DECORATE

a few small sprigs of mint

dried rose petals

3. Press the dough into the prepared pan as evenly as you can, then pierce it all over with a fork. Bake in the oven for 45 minutes, or until it is a rich golden-brown color. Let the cake cool in the pan, then transfer it to a plate. The cake will be fragile, so be careful.

4. Whip the cream until thick and quite firm, and stir in 1 tablespoon of the powdered sugar and rose water. Hull and halve the strawberries, then gently toss them in a bowl with the remaining powdered sugar and lemon juice. Let the sugar dissolve, then strain the strawberries.

5. Just before you are ready to serve (no sooner, because you don't want the shortcake to get soggy), pile the cream onto the shortcake and spoon the strawberries on top. Scatter with small sprigs of mint and rose petals.

HINNY CAKES WITH SUGARED BLUEBERRIES

HINNY CAKES ARE A TRADITIONAL ENGLISH SKILLET-COOKED TEATIME TREAT FROM NORTHUMBERLAND. THESE ARE TOPPED WITH BLUEBERRIES AND SUGAR, THEN LIGHTLY BROILED TO BRING OUT THE FULL FLAVOR OF THE FRUIT.

MAKES 10

1¼ cups self-rising flour
a pinch of salt
1 teaspoon baking powder
¼ teaspoon ground mace
¼ teaspoon ground cloves
5 tablespoons unsalted butter
2½ tablespoons ground rice
2 tablespoons superfine sugar

1. Sift the flour, salt, baking powder, mace, and cloves into a bowl. Dice 3 tablespoons of the butter and rub it into the flour mixture using your fingertips. When the mixture resembles fine breadcrumbs stir in the ground rice and sugar. Add the milk and mix to a fairly soft dough, using a round-bladed knife.

2. Set the dough out on a lightly floured work surface and knead very gently. Cut into 10 equal pieces. Lightly flour your hands, then shape each piece into a small flat cake.

generous ⅓ cup milk

2 tablespoons
   sunflower oil

TO FINISH

1½ to 2¼ cups
   blueberries

3½ tablespoons
   superfine sugar

lightly whipped cream

3. Melt 1 tablespoon of the remaining butter with half of the oil in a large heavy skillet over low heat. Place half of the cakes in the pan and fry gently for 3 to 4 minutes, or until golden underneath. Turn the cakes over and fry for another 3 to 4 minutes, or until cooked through. Transfer to a large cookie sheet. Melt the remaining butter with the remaining oil and fry the rest of the cakes the same way.

4. Preheat the broiler to medium. Spoon the blueberries onto the cakes, piling them up slightly in the center. Sprinkle with the sugar, then place under the broiler for about 2 minutes, watching closely, until the blueberries are bubbling and the edges of the cakes are lightly toasted. Serve immediately, with a dollop of whipped cream.

NOTE

IT IS ESSENTIAL TO COOK THESE CAKES ON VERY LOW HEAT. A HIGH TEMPERATURE WILL OVERCOOK THE CRUSTS WHILE THE CENTERS REMAIN RAW.

CINNAMON WAFERS WITH RASPBERRIES

FLAVORFUL RASPBERRIES ARE LAYERED WITH CREAM AND YOGURT BETWEEN CRISP HONEY AND CINNAMON WAFERS, THEN DUSTED GENEROUSLY WITH POWDERED SUGAR.

SERVES 8

3½ tablespoons unsalted butter (at room temperature)

¾ cup powdered sugar

¼ cup honey

heaping ½ cup all-purpose flour

1 teaspoon ground cinnamon

1 egg white, lightly beaten

1. Preheat the oven to 425°F. Line two large baking pans with wax paper.

2. Beat the butter in a bowl until very soft, then beat in the powdered sugar and honey. Sift the flour and cinnamon together and stir into the mixture with the egg white to make a smooth batter.

3. Drop 4 to 6 heaping teaspoonfuls of the mixture onto each baking pan, spacing them well apart, and spread out to 3-inch disks using the back of the spoon. Bake for 5 to 7 minutes, or until golden. Gently lift each one off of the baking pan with a metal spatula and transfer to a wire rack to cool

FOR THE FILLING

1¼ cups heavy cream

¾ cup Greek-style yogurt

2 tablespoons powdered sugar

2 tablespoons framboise or Kirsch (optional)

3 to 3½ cups raspberries

TO DECORATE

powdered sugar, for dusting

small mint leaves

and become crisp. The batter should make at least 24 wafers.

4. To make the filling, whip the cream until soft peaks form. Fold in the yogurt, sugar, and liqueur, if using.

5. To assemble, stack the wafers in threes, layering them together with the cream and raspberries. Dust generously with powdered sugar, decorate with a scattering of mint leaves, and serve immediately.

I WANT TO
HAVE A GOOD
BODY, BUT NOT
AS MUCH AS
I WANT DESSERT.

JASON LOVE

IF YOU'RE FEELING A LITTLE BIT DOWN, A LITTLE BIT OF KNEADING REALLY HELPS.

MARY BERRY

LAID-BACK
LOAVES

STICKY GINGERBREAD

STICKY BLACK MOLASSES AND SYRUPY STEM GINGER MAKE A GREAT TEAM IN THIS DELICIOUS ADAPTATION OF AN ALL-TIME OLD-FASHIONED FAVORITE. GRATED APPLES ADD EXTRA MOISTURE.

SERVES 12

- 1 large apple, weighing about 8 ounces
- 1 tablespoon lemon juice
- scant ½ cup molasses
- scant ½ cup light corn syrup
- 1 scant cup dark brown sugar
- 1½ sticks unsalted butter
- 1¾ cups all-purpose flour
- 1 cup whole-wheat flour
- 1 teaspoon ground pumpkin pie spice

1. Preheat the oven to 325°F. Grease the inside and line the bottom of a deep 7-inch square cake pan (see page 212).

2. Peel, core, and quarter the apple. Add the quarters to a bowl of water with the lemon juice to prevent the apple from discoloring.

3. Put the molasses, corn syrup, and sugar in a saucepan over low heat. Cut the butter into pieces and add to the pan. Heat gently until the butter melts, then let it cool slightly.

1½ teaspoons baking soda

2 eggs

5 ounces stem ginger pieces, thinly sliced, plus 3 tablespoons of syrup from the jar

4. Sift the all-purpose and whole-wheat flours, spice, and baking soda into a bowl. Grate three-quarters of the apple into the bowl and toss lightly in the flour. Add the melted syrup mixture, the eggs, and three-quarters of the ginger pieces. Beat thoroughly to combine.

5. Pour the batter into the prepared pan, spreading it into the corners. Using a vegetable peeler, pare the remaining apple into thin slices. Scatter the apple slices and remaining ginger pieces onto the surface of the gingerbread and press down lightly into the mixture using the tip of a knife. Bake for 1 hour and 20 minutes, or until firm to the touch. Let cool in the pan.

6. Remove the gingerbread from the pan and transfer it to a serving plate. Drizzle the ginger syrup evenly all over the surface.

NOTE

GINGERBREAD KEEPS WELL IN AN AIRTIGHT CONTAINER FOR UP TO A WEEK. FOR THE BEST FLAVOR, STORE FOR SEVERAL DAYS BEFORE EATING.

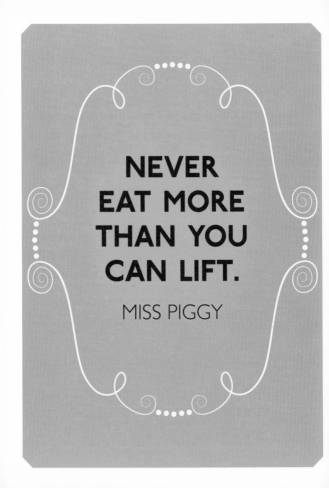

NEVER
EAT MORE
THAN YOU
CAN LIFT.

MISS PIGGY

MY WIFE
DRESSES
TO KILL. SHE
COOKS THE
SAME WAY.

HENNY
YOUNGMAN

ALMOND, CHOCOLATE, AND SWEET POTATO LOAF

This recipe uses puréed sweet potato to moisten and subtly flavor the loaf.

SERVES 8–10

½ pound sweet potatoes, peeled and cut into chunks

9 tablespoons butter, softened

¾ cup light brown sugar

1 teaspoon vanilla extract

2 eggs

1¼ cups self-rising flour

1½ tablespoons unsweetened cocoa powder

1 teaspoon ground pumpkin pie spice

½ teaspoon baking soda

1. Put the sweet potatoes in a pan of cold water, bring to a boil, and cook for 15 minutes, or until softened. Drain well, then mash with a potato masher.

2. Preheat the oven to 325°F. Grease an 8 x 4 x 3-inch (6-cup) loaf pan and line the bottom and long sides with a double thickness of wax paper, allowing the paper to hang over the sides of the pan (see page 212).

3. Put the butter, sugar, vanilla extract, and eggs in a bowl. Sift the flour, cocoa powder, mixed spice, and baking soda into the bowl. Add the milk and beat well until smooth and creamy.

2 tablespoons milk

4½ ounces milk chocolate, roughly chopped

¾ cup sliced almonds, lightly toasted

TO FINISH

1 tablespoon powdered sugar, for dusting

4. Stir in the mashed sweet potato, chopped chocolate, and ½ cup of the toasted almonds. Pour the batter into the prepared pan and level the surface. Scatter with the remaining almonds.

5. Bake for 1 to 1¼ hours, or until well risen and just firm to the touch. Leave in the pan for 10 minutes, then remove the loaf from the pan and transfer it to a wire rack to cool. Serve dusted with powdered sugar.

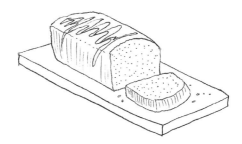

PUMPKIN TEACAKE WITH SPICED RAISINS

THIS IS AN OLD-FASHIONED TEACAKE, MADE MOIST BY THE ADDITION OF PUMPKIN. IT IS LOVELY SERVED STRAIGHT FROM THE OVEN, THOUGH YOU WILL NEED TO BE CAREFUL CUTTING IT AT THIS POINT BECAUSE IT WILL BE DIFFICULT TO SLICE.

SERVES 10–12

¾ cup raisins

scant ½ cup hot tea

1 cinnamon stick

1 piece of mace

1 long strip of lemon zest

1¼ cups all-purpose flour

2 teaspoons baking powder

½ teaspoon baking soda

¼ teaspoon freshly grated nutmeg

1. Place the raisins in a saucepan over high heat with the tea, cinnamon, mace, and lemon zest. Bring to a boil and remove from the heat. Set aside to infuse for at least 1 hour.

2. Preheat the oven to 325°F. Grease and line an 8 x 4 x 3-inch (6-cup) loaf pan (see page 212). In a bowl, sift together the flour, baking powder, baking soda, and nutmeg.

9 tablespoons
  unsalted butter,
  melted
¾ cup superfine sugar
2 large eggs
¾ cup cooked and
  mashed pumpkin

3. In another large bowl, beat together the butter and sugar. Add the eggs, followed by the pumpkin, then drain the raisin mixture and add it to the bowl. Gradually incorporate the flour mixture until well combined.

4. Pour the batter into the prepared loaf pan and bake for about 1 hour, or until golden brown and a skewer inserted in the center comes out clean. Let cool in the pan before transferring to a serving plate.

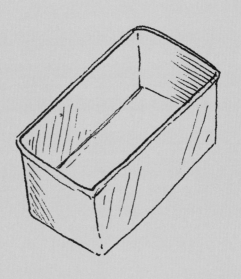

YOU HAVE
TO EAT TO COOK.
YOU CAN'T BE A
GOOD COOK AND
BE A NON-EATER.
I THINK EATING IS
THE SECRET TO
GOOD COOKING.

JULIA CHILD

APPLE, GOLDEN RAISIN, AND APPLE CIDER SLICES

THIS SIMPLE SPONGE CAKE IS RICHLY FILLED WITH SWEET, FRAGRANT APPLES AND GOLDEN RAISINS AND BAKED ON A PUFF PASTRY BASE.

MAKES 12

8 ounces ready-made puff pastry

3 apples

1 tablespoon lemon juice

1½ sticks unsalted butter, softened

¾ cup + 2 tablespoons superfine sugar

1¾ cups self-rising flour

½ teaspoon baking powder

3 eggs

3 tablespoons apple cider

1. Preheat the oven to 400°F. Lightly dampen a large cookie sheet. Roll out the pastry thinly on a lightly floured work surface to an 11-inch square and place on the cookie sheet. Pierce the surface all over with a fork and bake for 10 minutes until risen. Lower the oven temperature to 350°F.

2. Lightly grease a shallow 9-inch square baking pan. Cut the pastry to fit the bottom of the pan, then carefully press it into position.

½ cup golden raisins

2 teaspoons
powdered sugar

TO FINISH

powdered sugar, for
dusting

3. Peel, core, and slice one of the apples. Add the slices to a bowl of water with 1 teaspoon of the lemon juice. Core and slice the remaining apples (do not peel them) and place in a separate bowl with the remaining lemon juice.

4. Cream the butter and sugar together in a bowl until pale and creamy. Sift the flour and baking powder into a bowl. Add the eggs and apple cider and beat well until smooth. Drain the peeled apple slices and stir into the mixture along with the golden raisins. Spoon the mixture onto the baked pastry and level the surface.

5. Drain the unpeeled apple slices and arrange on top of the filling. Dust with the powdered sugar and bake for 45 to 50 minutes, or until just firm. Let cool in the pan for 15 minutes.

6. Dust the cake once again with powdered sugar, cut it into slices, and serve warm.

DATE AND BANANA LOAF

THIS SIMPLE TEA BREAD HAS A BEAUTIFULLY MOIST TEXTURE AND A
DISTINCTIVE BANANA TASTE, ALONG WITH A SLIGHT TANG. LAYERS OF
PURÉED DATES ADD AN EXTRA DEPTH OF FLAVOR.

SERVES 8–10

1½ cups pitted
dried dates

zest and juice
of 1 lemon

2 ripe bananas

1½ sticks unsalted
butter, softened

¾ cup superfine sugar

2 eggs

1¾ cups self-rising
flour

½ teaspoon baking
powder

1. Preheat the oven to 325°F. Grease and
line an 8 x 4 x 1½-inch (5-cup) loaf pan
(see page 212).

2. Set aside 4 of the dates. Place the
remainder in a small heavy saucepan and
add the lemon zest and juice and a scant
¼ cup of water. Bring to a boil, reduce
the heat, and simmer gently for 5 minutes
until the dates are soft and pulpy. Blend the
mixture in a food processor or blender
until smooth, or mash together in a bowl
with a fork.

3. In another bowl, mash the bananas until completely smooth. Cream the butter and sugar together in a bowl until light and fluffy. Add the mashed bananas and the eggs. Sift the flour and baking powder into the bowl and beat until thoroughly combined.

4. Spoon one-third of the banana mixture into the prepared loaf pan and level the top. Spread half of the blended dates onto the surface. Repeat the layers again, then cover with the remaining banana mixture.

5. Cut the reserved dates into thin slices and scatter them over the surface. Bake for 1 to 1¼ hours, or until well risen and firm to the touch. Leave in the pan for 15 minutes, then transfer to a wire rack to cool. Store in an airtight container for up to a week.

TIP

THE DATE PURÉE NEEDS TO BE SIMILAR IN CONSISTENCY TO THE BANANA MIXTURE. IF IT SEEMS TOO THICK, BEAT IN A LITTLE WATER.

HONEY, VANILLA, AND BLUEBERRY LOAF

THE PAIRING OF HONEY AND VANILLA IS ONE OF THE MOST
COMFORTING COMBINATIONS.

SERVES 8–10

2¼ sticks unsalted
  butter, softened
¾ cup superfine sugar
¼ cup honey
3 large eggs
scant 2½ cups self-
  rising flour
1 teaspoon vanilla
  extract
1 tablespoon milk
1¼ cups blueberries
2 tablespoons
  superfine sugar

1. Preheat the oven to 325°F. Grease and
line an 8 x 4 x 3-inch (6-cup) loaf pan (see
page 212).

2. Beat the butter until very soft and then
add the sugar and honey. Cream together
until the mixture is very soft, light, and
fluffy.

3. Beat in the eggs one at a time, folding
in a tablespoon of the flour after each
addition. Gently fold in the rest of the flour,
then mix in the vanilla extract and milk.
The batter should be slightly stiffer than a
dropping consistency.

4. Scrape half of the batter into the prepared loaf pan. Fold half of the blueberries through the remaining batter and spoon this on top. Scatter the remaining blueberries on top of the loaf and sprinkle with the superfine sugar.

5. Bake for about 1 hour, or until a skewer inserted in the center comes out clean. Let cool in the pan before transferring to a serving plate.

CHERRY STREUSEL SLICE

Crumbly, mildly spiced, and pleasantly sweet, serve this delightfully mouthwatering cake with a dollop of lightly whipped cream.

SERVES 8

- 2 15-ounce cans pitted dark sweet cherries in juice
- 2 teaspoons cornstarch
- 1 teaspoon vanilla extract
- 2 cups self-rising flour
- 1 teaspoon ground cinnamon
- zest of ½ lemon
- 1½ sticks unsalted butter
- heaping ¾ cup superfine sugar

1. Drain the cherries, reserving a generous ¹/₃ cup of the juice. Blend a little of the juice with the cornstarch in a small pan. Add the remaining juice along with the vanilla extract and bring to a boil, stirring. Add the cherries and cook, stirring constantly, for another minute, or until they are thickly coated in the syrup. Set aside to cool.

2. Grease an 8 x 4 x 3-inch (6-cup) loaf pan and line the bottom and long sides with a double thickness of wax paper, allowing it to hang over the sides of the pan (see page 212).

3. Preheat the oven to 350°F. Place the flour, cinnamon, and lemon zest in a food

½ cup ground
  almonds
1 egg

TO FINISH
1 tablespoon
  powdered sugar,
  for dusting

processor. Cut the butter into small pieces
and add it to the flour mixture. Process it
until the mixture starts to cling together.
Add the sugar and ground almonds, and
process briefly until the mixture resembles
coarse crumbs. (Or rub the butter into
the flour, cinnamon, and lemon zest using
your fingertips, then stir in the sugar and
ground almonds.) Set aside ¾ cup of the
mixture for the topping. Add the egg to the
remaining mixture and combine to make a
fairly soft paste.

4. Use half of the paste to thickly line
the bottom of the prepared pan. Roll out
the remainder and cut into strips about
1 inch wide. Use these to line the sides of
the pan, pressing them to fit around the
corners and bottom, eliminating the gaps.

5. Spoon the cherry filling into the center
and scatter evenly with the reserved
topping mixture. Bake for 40 to 45
minutes, or until the topping is pale golden.
Let cool in the pan.

6. Loosen the edges at the end of the pan, then carefully lift the cake out, using the wax paper to help you. Dust with powdered sugar to serve.

LAID-BACK LOAVES

YOU DON'T COME INTO COOKING TO GET RICH.

GORDON
RAMSAY

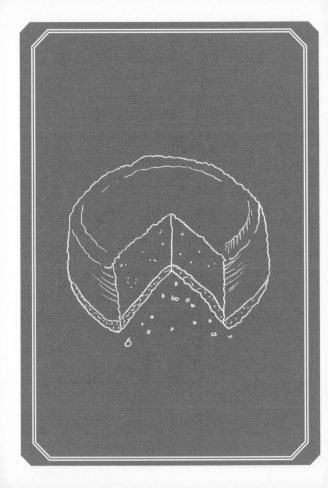

PEACEFUL PUDDINGS and DESSERTS

ALMOND AND AMARETTI CHEESECAKE

THIS LIGHT, CREAMY CHEESECAKE IS TOPPED WITH CRUSHED AMARETTI COOKIES AND SERVED WITH A NECTARINE COMPOTE ON THE SIDE.

SERVES 8

1¼ cups graham cracker crumbs

¼ cup ground almonds

5 tablespoons unsalted butter, melted

FOR THE FILLING

heaping ½ cup mascarpone cheese

½ cup ricotta cheese

¼ cup superfine sugar

2 eggs, separated

½ teaspoon vanilla extract

1. Make the cheesecake the day before you wish to serve it because the texture improves a great deal overnight. Preheat the oven to 300°F. Grease and line an 8-inch round springform cake pan (see page 212).

2. Place the graham cracker crumbs, ground almonds, and melted butter in a bowl and stir to combine. Press the mixture evenly all over the bottom and about ¼ inch up the inside of the pan. Cover the crust loosely with plastic wrap and let chill in the fridge while you make the filling.

1 tablespoon cornstarch

scant ½ cup crème fraîche or sour cream

1¾ ounces amaretti cookies

FOR THE COMPOTE

4 ripe nectarines

¾ cup white wine

heaping ⅓ cup superfine sugar

1 vanilla bean

3. Place the mascarpone and ricotta cheeses in a large bowl and beat together well. Add the sugar, egg yolks, vanilla extract, and cornstarch and beat again, then fold in the crème fraîche or sour cream. In another bowl, beat the egg whites until soft peaks form. Stir one-third of the egg whites into the cheesecake mixture, then carefully fold in the rest.

4. Pour the mixture into the prepared crust. Crumble the amaretti cookies into chunky crumbs and scatter them on top. Bake in the oven for 1½ hours, or until just firm to the touch. Turn off the oven but leave the cheesecake inside the oven to cool.

5. Meanwhile, make the nectarine compote. Halve the nectarines, remove the stones, then cut the flesh into quarters. Place in a saucepan with the wine, sugar, vanilla bean, and ¾ cup of water. Bring slowly to a boil, then reduce the heat, cover, and simmer very gently for about

5 minutes, or until the nectarines are just tender. Set the mixture aside to cool, then discard the vanilla bean. Chill the compote in the fridge for several hours.

6. Serve the cheesecake, cut into wedges, with a generous spoonful of the compote on the side.

RECIPE: A SERIES
OF STEP-BY-STEP
INSTRUCTIONS
FOR PREPARING
INGREDIENTS YOU
FORGOT TO BUY,
IN UTENSILS YOU
DON'T OWN, TO MAKE
A DISH THE DOG
WOULDN'T EAT.

ANON

CHOCOLATE, WALNUT, AND MAPLE PUDDING

THESE PRETTY INDIVIDUAL PUDDINGS ARE MADE FROM A MIXTURE OF EGGS, COCOA POWDER, WALNUTS, AND GROUND ALMONDS, WHICH GIVES THE PUDDINGS A LIGHT, SOUFFLÉ-LIKE TEXTURE.

SERVES 8

1¼ sticks unsalted butter, softened

1 scant cup light brown sugar

¼ teaspoon ground nutmeg

¼ cup all-purpose flour

¼ cup unsweetened cocoa powder

5 eggs, separated

1¼ cups ground almonds

½ cup breadcrumbs

½ cup chopped walnuts

1. Preheat the oven to 350°F. Grease 8 individual 4-ounce (3-inch) ramekins. Line the bottoms with wax paper.

2. In a bowl, cream the butter together with ¼ cup of the sugar and the nutmeg. Beat until light and fluffy, then sift the flour and cocoa powder into the bowl. Add the egg yolks, ground almonds, breadcrumbs, and nuts, and stir until just combined.

3. Beat the egg whites until stiff, then gradually beat in the remaining sugar. Using a large metal spoon, fold one-quarter of the egg-white mixture into the chocolate mixture to loosen it. Gently fold in the remaining egg whites.

PEACEFUL PUDDINGS AND DESSERTS

TO SERVE

crème fraîche or sour
  cream

maple syrup

chopped walnuts, for
  scattering

4. Spoon the pudding mixture into the prepared ramekins, filling them no more than two-thirds full.

5. Stand the ramekins in a roasting pan and pour in boiling water to a depth of ¼ inch. Cover the pan completely with foil and bake for 30 minutes, or until the puddings feel firm.

6. Loosen the edge of each pudding with a knife and invert onto warmed serving plates. Place a spoonful of crème fraîche or sour cream beside each pudding. Drizzle all over with maple syrup and scatter with chopped walnuts to serve.

SUMMER PUDDING

THIS QUINTESSENTIAL BRITISH PUDDING NEEDS NOTHING MORE THAN A DOLLOP OF CREAM TO GO WITH IT. IT'S EXTREMELY EASY TO MAKE AND—LIKE ALL GREAT DINNER-PARTY DESSERTS—CAN BE MADE THE NIGHT BEFORE, READY TO INVERT ONTO A SERVING PLATE WHEN REQUIRED.

SERVES 6–8

3 cups raspberries

2 cups red currants

2 cups black currants

scant ½ cup superfine sugar

8 large slices of white bread, ¼-inch thick, crusts removed (see note)

1. Put the raspberries in a saucepan with the red and black currants, sugar, and 3 tablespoons of water. Bring to a gentle simmer over low heat, then cook gently for 3 to 4 minutes, or until the juices begin to run. Remove from the heat and set aside.

2. Cut out a disk of bread from one of the slices to fit the bottom of an 8-inch (6-cup) pudding bowl. Cut the remaining slices in half lengthwise.

3. Arrange the bread slices around the side of the pudding bowl, overlapping them slightly at the bottom, so they fit neatly

TO DECORATE

sprigs of red currants
lemon balm or
  mint leaves

TO SERVE

heavy cream

and tightly together. Set the disk of bread in the bottom.

4. Spoon a scant ½ cup of the fruit juice into a pitcher and set aside. Spoon the remaining fruit and its juice into the bread-lined pudding bowl. Cover completely with the remaining bread slices, trimming them to fit.

5. Cover the pudding with a saucer that just fits inside the top of the pudding bowl, then set a 4½-pound weight on the saucer (or use a couple of unopened cans of food from the cupboard). Chill the pudding in the fridge overnight.

6. To serve the pudding, remove the weight and saucer and invert a serving plate over the pudding bowl. Hold the two very firmly together and turn them over all at once. Give them a firm shake (up and down, rather than side to side), then carefully lift the pudding bowl off of the pudding.

NOTE

CHOOSE A GOOD-QUALITY, DENSELY TEXTURED LARGE WHITE LOAF, PREFERABLY ONE DAY OLD.

7. Spoon the reserved juice all over the pudding and decorate it with sprigs of red currants and lemon balm or mint leaves. Serve, cut into wedges, with plenty of cream.

COOKING REQUIRES CONFIDENT GUESSWORK AND IMPROVISATION, EXPERIMENTATION, AND SUBSTITUTION, DEALING WITH FAILURE AND UNCERTAINTY IN A CREATIVE WAY.

PAUL THEROUX

New York Cheesecake

THIS IS A CLASSIC OVEN-BAKED NEW YORK CHEESECAKE. THE TEXTURE IMPROVES REMARKABLY IF THE CHEESECAKE IS LEFT TO CHILL OVERNIGHT IN THE FRIDGE.

SERVES 8–10

1¼ sticks unsalted butter, melted

2½ cups graham cracker crumbs

1 teaspoon ground cinnamon

FOR THE FILLING

2½ cups regular cream cheese

1 heaping cup soft light brown sugar

3 eggs

1 egg yolk

¾ cup sour cream

1. Place the melted butter, graham cracker crumbs, and cinnamon in a bowl and stir until combined. Press evenly into the bottom of an 8-inch round springform pan. Chill for about 1 hour until set.

2. Preheat the oven to 350°F. Using an electric mixer, beat the cream cheese until smooth. Continue to beat the mixture as you add the sugar and then the eggs and egg yolk one by one. Slowly spoon in the sour cream, then stir in the vanilla extract and the lemon zest. Pour the filling onto the graham cracker crust and smooth the surface.

1 teaspoon vanilla
   extract

zest of 1 lemon

FOR THE TOPPING

¾ cup Marsala wine

juice of ½ lemon

scant ½ cup superfine
   sugar

scant ½ cup raisins

3. Completely seal the pan in a layer of foil. Set the pan in a large roasting pan and pour boiling water around it, so it comes about halfway up the sides of the pan. Bake for about 50 minutes. The cheesecake should feel set but still be a little wobbly. Remove from the oven. Once it has cooled, place the pan in the fridge to chill overnight.

4. Meanwhile, make the raisin syrup topping. Put all of the ingredients in a saucepan and simmer until the syrup has reduced a little. Allow to cool, then chill in the fridge overnight. To serve, remove the sides of the springform pan, cut the cheesecake into serving slices, and drizzle some raisin syrup over each slice.

BREAD AND BUTTER PUDDING

LIGHT, FLAKY CROISSANTS REPLACE THE BREAD THAT IS NORMALLY USED IN THIS TRADITIONAL PUDDING. SOAK THE GOLDEN RAISINS IN A LITTLE BRANDY TO PLUMP THEM UP IF YOU LIKE.

SERVES 6

4 large croissants (see note)

5 tablespoons unsalted butter (at room temperature)

½ cup golden raisins

FOR THE CUSTARD

1¼ cups milk (at room temperature)

1¼ cups heavy cream (at room temperature)

1 vanilla bean, split

6 egg yolks

½ cup + 2 tablespoons superfine sugar

1. Preheat the oven to 350°F. Grease a shallow 1½-quart baking dish.

2. Slice the croissants thickly, then spread with the butter. Arrange the croissant slices, buttered-side up and overlapping, in the prepared dish. Scatter with golden raisins as you go.

3. To make the custard, pour the milk and cream into a saucepan. Add the vanilla bean and place over very low heat for about 5 minutes, or until the mixture is almost boiling and well flavored with vanilla.

TO FINISH

1 tablespoon
 powdered sugar,
 for dusting
heavy cream

4. Meanwhile, in a large bowl, beat together the egg yolks and superfine sugar until light and foamy. Strain the flavored milk into the egg mixture, beating all the time.

5. Pour the egg mixture evenly all over the croissants. Place the baking dish in a large roasting pan and pour enough boiling water into the pan to come halfway up the sides of the dish. Bake for 45 to 50 minutes, or until the custard is softly set and the top is crisp and golden brown.

6. Remove from the oven and leave the baking dish sitting in the water in the roasting pan until just warm. Dust with the powdered sugar and serve with cream.

NOTE

THE CROISSANTS ARE BETTER USED WHEN SLIGHTLY STALE. LEAVE THEM IN A COOL PLACE FOR A DAY OR TWO TO DRY AND GROW FIRM BEFORE SLICING.

CHOCOLATE BREAD AND BUTTER PUDDING

THIS RECIPE HAS ALL THE COMFORTING QUALITIES OF A TRADITIONAL BREAD AND BUTTER PUDDING. THE BONUS HERE IS THE DARK, GOOEY CHOCOLATE SAUCE THAT LURKS IN GENEROUS POCKETS AND OOZES INTO THE SPICED VANILLA CUSTARD.

SERVES 6

7 ounces baking chocolate (at least 70% cocoa solids)

5 tablespoons unsalted butter

8 ounces fruit loaf or light tea bread

1 teaspoon vanilla extract

½ teaspoon ground cinnamon

3 eggs

2 tablespoons superfine sugar

2½ cups milk

1. Lightly grease the inside of a shallow 1½-quart baking dish. Break up the chocolate and add it to a heatproof bowl set over a pan of barely simmering water (see page 218). Add 2 tablespoons of the butter. Let melt, then stir lightly.

2. Cut the fruit bread into thin slices and arrange one-third of the slices, overlapping, in the prepared baking dish. Spread with half of the chocolate sauce. Arrange half of the remaining bread in the dish and spread this layer with the remaining sauce. Finally arrange the last of the bread slices on top.

TO FINISH

unsweetened cocoa powder and powdered sugar, for dusting

3. Melt the remaining butter. Remove from the heat and stir in the vanilla extract, cinnamon, eggs, sugar, and milk. Beat thoroughly, then pour the mixture all over the bread. Let stand for 1 hour until the bread has softened. Preheat the oven to 350°F.

4. Bake the pudding for 45 to 55 minutes, or until the custard has set and the bread is deep golden brown. Let stand for 5 minutes, then dust with cocoa powder and powdered sugar to serve.

NOTE

USE A TEA BREAD THAT'S JUST LIGHTLY SPECKLED WITH FRUITS; OTHERWISE, THE PUDDING WILL BE TOO HEAVY.

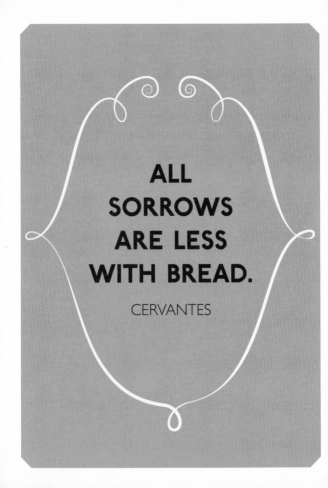

ALL
SORROWS
ARE LESS
WITH BREAD.

CERVANTES

WHEN
BAKING, FOLLOW
DIRECTIONS.
WHEN COOKING,
GO BY YOUR
OWN TASTE.

LAIKO BAHRS

SPICED RAISIN PUDDINGS WITH DEMERARA LEMON SAUCE

FEW OF US WITH A PASSION FOR DESSERT CAN RESIST A TRADITIONAL BRITISH PUDDING, ALL HOT AND STEAMING. THIS ONE WON'T DISAPPOINT.

MAKES 8

½ ounces stem ginger in syrup

1½ sticks unsalted butter, softened

¾ cups + 2 tablespoons superfine sugar

3 eggs, lightly beaten

1¾ cups self-rising flour

1½ teaspoons baking powder

1 teaspoon ground pumpkin pie spice

1. Preheat the oven to 350°F. Lightly grease the bottom and insides of 8 individual 4-ounce (3-inch) metal custard bowls or ramekins. Mince the stem ginger and set aside.

2. In a large bowl, cream together the butter and sugar until light and fluffy. Add the beaten eggs, a little at a time, beating well after each addition and adding a little of the flour each time to stop the mixture from curdling.

3. Sift the remaining flour, baking powder, and the spices into the bowl. Add the

½ teaspoon ground
    cinnamon
½ cup raisins
a little milk

FOR THE SAUCE

5 tablespoons
    unsalted butter
1 cup Demerara sugar
zest and juice of
    2 small lemons

TO SERVE

heavy cream or crème
    fraîche

raisins and minced ginger and gradually
fold them all in, using a large metal spoon.
Stir in enough milk to give a soft, dropping
consistency.

4. Divide the mixture among the
prepared pans and level the surfaces. Stand
each one in a roasting pan and pour in
enough boiling water around the pans to
reach a depth of ¼ inch. Cover the entire
roasting pan with foil. Bake for 40 to 45
minutes, or until the puddings have risen
and feel firm to the touch.

5. Meanwhile, make the sauce. Melt the
butter in a small saucepan over medium
heat. Add the sugar and heat gently for 2
to 3 minutes, or until bubbling. Add the
lemon zest and juice and cook gently until
you have a buttery syrup.

6. Loosen around the edge of each
pudding with a knife, then transfer each to
a warmed serving plate. Pour a little sauce
over each pudding and add a dollop of
cream or crème fraîche to serve.

Apple Bramble Pudding

APPLES, BLACKBERRIES, AND RASPBERRIES ARE COOKED IN A SYRUPY BUTTER, THEN LAYERED WITH SOFT BREAD AND BAKED TO A GOLDEN CRUST. SERVE WITH CREAMY CUSTARD.

SERVES 6

9 tablespoons unsalted butter

½ cup Demerara sugar

1½ pounds apples

2 tablespoons lemon juice

2½ cups blackberries

1¾ cups raspberries

1 heaping cup red or black currants

1 tablespoon oil

6 slices traditional white bread, crusts removed

a little Demerara sugar, for sprinkling

1. Preheat the oven to 400°F. Lightly grease a 2-quart baking dish. Melt 3½ tablespoons of the butter in a large saucepan. Add the sugar and stir until beginning to dissolve.

2. Peel, core, and thickly slice the apples and add them to the pan. Cook gently, stirring frequently, for 5 minutes. Add the lemon juice, blackberries, raspberries, and red or black currants. Toss lightly to combine.

3. Spoon half of the fruit mixture into the baking dish. Melt the remaining butter in a skillet with the oil, add half of the bread slices, and fry until beginning to brown on the underside. Remove with a spatula and place the slices, browned-side up, on top of the fruit in the baking dish. (Reserve the butter and oil in the skillet.)

4. Spread the rest of the fruits and juices all over the bread. Cut the remaining bread into triangles and arrange on top of the fruit in the dish. Brush liberally with the reserved butter and oil, then sprinkle with Demerara sugar. Bake for about 25 minutes, or until the bread topping is deep golden.

VARIATIONS

VIRTUALLY ANY COMBINATION OF SOFT FRUITS CAN BE USED IN THIS PUDDING, BUT AVOID TOO MANY BLACK CURRANTS BECAUSE THEIR FLAVOR WILL DOMINATE.

THE BEST COOKING IS THAT WHICH TAKES INTO ACCOUNT THE PRODUCTS OF THE SEASON.

AUGUSTE ESCOFFIER

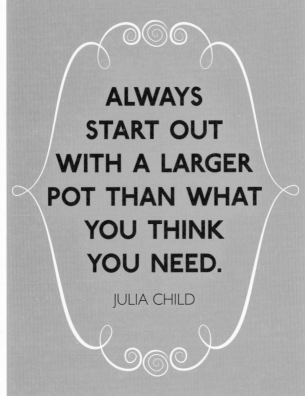

ALWAYS
START OUT
WITH A LARGER
POT THAN WHAT
YOU THINK
YOU NEED.

JULIA CHILD

Sticky Date and Orange Pudding

Flavored with oranges, dates, and flecks of white chocolate, the light-textured spongy pudding is topped with an indulgent toffee sauce. Serve with custard or light cream.

SERVES 6

1 cup pitted dates, roughly chopped

⅔ cup fresh orange juice

5 tablespoons unsalted butter, softened

¾ cup light brown sugar

2 eggs

1 cup + 2 tablespoons self-rising flour

2 tablespoons unsweetened cocoa powder

½ teaspoon baking soda

1. Butter a 1½-quart pudding bowl and line the bottom with a disk of wax paper. Place the dates in a saucepan with the orange juice. Bring to a boil, reduce the heat, and simmer gently for 5 minutes. Set aside to cool while preparing the pudding.

2. Add the butter, sugar, and eggs to a large bowl. Sift the flour, cocoa powder, and baking soda into the bowl and beat well until evenly combined.

3. Using a slotted spoon, remove and reserve one-third of the date pieces from the saucepan. Add the remaining dates and orange juice to the pudding mixture

zest of 1 orange

1¾ ounces white
chocolate, roughly
chopped

FOR THE SAUCE

⅔ cup light brown
sugar

5 tablespoons
unsalted butter

¼ cup heavy cream

1 tablespoon lemon
juice

TO SERVE

homemade custard
(see page 216) or
light cream

NOTE

IF YOU DON'T HAVE
A STEAMER, REST THE
PUDDING BOWL ON
AN UPSIDE-DOWN
SAUCER IN A LARGE
SAUCEPAN OVER
MEDIUM HEAT. ADD
ENOUGH BOILING
WATER TO THE PAN
TO COME HALFWAY
UP THE SIDES OF THE
PUDDING BOWL.

---

along with the orange zest and chopped
chocolate. Stir well, then pour into the
prepared pudding bowl.

4. Cover the bowl with two sheets of
wax paper and a single sheet of foil. Tie
some kitchen string under the rim to hold
the cover in place. Set in a steamer and
add boiling water. Cover and let steam for
2 hours. Replenish with more boiling water
as necessary during cooking.

5. Meanwhile, make the sauce. Put the
sugar, butter, and cream in a small pan.
Heat gently until the sugar dissolves, then
stir in the reserved dates and lemon juice.
Let boil for 1 minute.

6. Remove the pudding from the steamer
and discard the paper and foil. Carefully
invert the bowl onto a serving plate and lift
it off of the pudding. Pour the toffee sauce
onto the pudding to coat evenly. Serve any
remaining sauce in a separate pitcher, along
with custard or light cream.

CHRISTMAS PUDDING

A RICH AND STICKY TRADITIONAL FIGGY PUDDING PACKED WITH
DRIED FRUITS PLUMPED UP WITH STRONG DARK BEER AND BRANDY.
THIS PUDDING IS KEPT MOIST WITH BUTTER INSTEAD OF SUET.

**MAKES 2
PUDDINGS; EACH
SERVES 8–10**

1¼ cups dried mixed
fruit

¾ cup dried dates

1¾ cups golden
raisins

1¾ cups seedless
raisins

⅔ cup strong dark
beer

¼ cup brandy, dark
rum, or Armagnac

zest and juice of
1 lemon

zest and juice
of 1 orange

¾ cup ready-to-eat
dried figs

1. Place the dried mixed fruit, dates,
golden raisins, and raisins in a shallow bowl
and add the strong dark beer and brandy.
Add the lemon and orange juice. Stir
well, cover, and let soak overnight, stirring
occasionally.

2. The next day, drain the soaked fruit
and reserve any juices. Roughly chop the
fruit (discarding any pits you come across),
figs, and ginger, and place in a large bowl.

3. Stir in the almonds, breadcrumbs, sugar,
and spices. Grate the butter and fold it
into the mixture. Beat the eggs with any
liquid remaining from the soaked fruit and
stir into the mixture with the lemon and
orange zest.

4½ ounces stem ginger

1½ cups whole unblanched almonds

3 cups fresh brown breadcrumbs

1¼ cups dark brown sugar

1 teaspoon grated nutmeg

1 teaspoon ground cinnamon

1 teaspoon ground ginger

1½ sticks unsalted butter, chilled

4 large eggs

TO SERVE

6 tablespoons brandy

brandy or rum butter

pouring custard (see page 216)

4. Butter two 5-cup pudding bowls. Divide the batter equally between the two and smooth the surface. Cover with a pleated double layer of wax paper, and top with a pleated sheet of foil (pleating allows the pudding to expand while cooking). Tie some kitchen string under the rim to hold the cover in place and use more string to make a handle to help lift the puddings out of the pans later.

5. Set the pudding bowls in one or two large saucepans and pour in enough boiling water to come halfway up the sides of the bowls. Cover and steam for 6 hours, checking the water level and replenishing with boiling water as necessary. Do not let the pans boil dry. Cool completely, then wrap in fresh wax paper and foil and store in a cool place until needed.

6. To serve, steam each pudding as before for 2 hours. Remove the paper and foil and invert onto a warmed serving platter. Heat the brandy in a small pan and pour it onto the puddings. Ignite with a match or taper and tilt the plate from time to time to burn off all of the alcohol. Serve with brandy or rum butter, or thin custard.

**ANYBODY
WHO BELIEVES
THAT THE WAY TO
A MAN'S HEART
IS THROUGH HIS
STOMACH FLUNKED
GEOGRAPHY.**

ROBERT BYRNE

SERENE
SPONGE
CAKES

Marbled Lemon Flower Cake

This is a very pretty cake. The inside is swirled with pink and yellow, and the lemon frosting provides the perfect backdrop for a display of edible flowers.

SERVES 8

2 cups all-purpose flour

1½ teaspoons baking powder

½ teaspoon baking soda

9 tablespoons unsalted butter

1 cup superfine sugar

3 eggs

1 scant cup buttermilk

1 teaspoon vanilla extract

zest of 1 lemon

1 tablespoon lemon juice

1. Preheat the oven to 350°F. Grease and flour a 10-inch Bundt pan with a depth of 2 inches (see page 213). Sift the flour with the baking powder and baking soda to combine thoroughly.

2. Beat the butter with an electric stand mixer until soft, then add the sugar. Continue to beat until very light and fluffy. Add the eggs one at a time, alternating with tablespoons of the flour mixture to stop the wet mixture from curdling, then gently fold in the rest of the flour mixture. Stir in the buttermilk and vanilla extract.

1 teaspoon rose
water

a few drops of pink
food coloring

FOR THE FROSTING

2 tablespoons lemon
juice

2 cups powdered
sugar, sifted

TO DECORATE

a selection of edible
fresh, dried, or
crystallized flowers

3. Pour two-thirds of the batter into another bowl and stir in the zest and lemon juice to combine. Stir the rose water and pink food coloring into the batter remaining in the first bowl.

4. Pour the lemon batter into the prepared cake pan and spread it out evenly. Spoon the rose batter on top, then smooth it down and swirl through with a metal spatula to create a marbled effect.

5. Bake for about 25 minutes, or until well risen and firm to the touch. Remove from the oven, transfer to a wire rack, and let cool completely.

6. Meanwhile, make the frosting. Beat the lemon juice into the powdered sugar and gradually add cold water, half a teaspoon at a time, until it is the desired consistency—you should be able to drizzle it, rather than spread it.

7. When the cake has completely cooled, remove it from the pan and transfer to a serving dish. Drizzle the frosting all over it and decorate with the flowers to serve.

A CAKE IS A VERY GOOD TEST OF AN OVEN: IF IT BROWNS TOO MUCH ON ONE SIDE AND NOT ON THE OTHER, IT'S NOT YOUR FAULT—YOU NEED TO HAVE YOUR OVEN CHECKED.

DELIA SMITH

ALMOND ANGEL CAKE

THIS CAKE HAS A LIGHT, BOUNCY CONSISTENCY, WHICH IS GIVEN TEXTURE BY THE ADDITION OF GROUND ALMONDS.

SERVES 8

½ cup all-purpose flour

2 tablespoons cornstarch

¾ cup superfine sugar

5 egg whites

½ teaspoon cream of tartar

½ teaspoon vanilla extract

¼ teaspoon almond extract

1 teaspoon lemon juice

¾ cup ground almonds

1. Preheat the oven to 350°F. Grease a shallow 10-inch Bundt pan and then dust the inside surface with flour (see page 213).

2. Mix together the all-purpose flour and cornstarch, then sift the mixture at least three times so the ingredients are well combined and aerated. Add half of the superfine sugar and sift the mixture one last time.

3. Beat the egg whites together until they form soft peaks. Add the cream of tartar, then gradually add the remaining sugar, beating constantly, until the mixture is stiff and glossy. Stir in the vanilla extract, almond extract, and lemon juice.

TO SERVE

½ cup sliced almonds

½ pound fresh summer fruits (a mixture of strawberries, raspberries, and blueberries)

2 tablespoons powdered sugar

whipped cream or crème fraîche

4. Using a large metal spoon fold in the flour mixture and the ground almonds.

5. Spoon the batter into the prepared pan. Bake for 30 to 35 minutes, or until golden brown with a springy texture. Let cake cool in the pan for 10 minutes, then remove it from the pan and transfer it to a plate.

6. Toast the sliced almonds in a dry skillet until they turn light brown.

7. To assemble the cake, pile the summer fruits into the hollow center of the angel cake. Dust everything with powdered sugar and scatter with the sliced almonds. Serve with whipped cream or crème fraîche.

MAPLE SYRUP AND PECAN CAKE

THIS IS AN EXCELLENT CAKE FOR ENJOYING IN THE FALL. MAKE SURE THE PEAR ISN'T TOO RIPE; OTHERWISE, IT WILL MAKE THE CAKE SOGGY.

SERVES 8–10

2¾ cups all-purpose flour

2 teaspoons baking powder

½ teaspoon baking soda

2 sticks unsalted butter, softened

1¼ cups light brown sugar

4 eggs

½ cup maple syrup

1 tablespoon milk

½ cup pecans, finely chopped

1 firm pear, peeled, cored, and finely chopped

1. Preheat the oven to 350°F. Grease the insides and line the bottoms of two deep 8-inch round cake pans (see page 212). Sift together the all-purpose flour, baking powder, and baking soda.

2. Beat together the butter and sugar until soft, fluffy, and a very pale golden brown. Beat in the eggs, one at a time, alternating with spoonfuls of the flour mixture to stop the wet mixture from curdling, then fold in the rest of the flour mixture with a large metal spoon.

3. Drizzle in the maple syrup and the milk and stir until you have a good dropping consistency. Add the pecans and the chopped pear and stir just until combined.

4. Pour the batter into the prepared pans and bake for about 30 minutes, or until well risen, golden brown, and firm to the touch. Let cool for 10 minutes before removing the cakes from their pans and transferring to a wire rack.

5. To make the topping, beat the mascarpone cheese until soft and fluffy. In a separate bowl, beat the heavy cream until thick and doubled in volume. Gently beat the mascarpone cheese and the heavy cream together, then add the maple syrup and vanilla extract and stir to combine.

6. To assemble, place one cake onto a serving dish and spread one-third of the topping onto it. Stack the other cake on top. Use the remaining topping to cover the top and sides of the entire cake. Decorate with the pecan halves.

CARROT CAKE WITH MASCARPONE TOPPING

IN THIS VERSION OF CARROT CAKE, BRAZIL NUTS REPLACE THE MORE FAMILIAR WALNUTS, AND MILD, CREAMY MASCARPONE FROSTING PROVIDES A DELICIOUSLY SMOOTH TOPPING.

SERVE 8–10

2 sticks unsalted butter, softened

1 cup + 2 tablespoons superfine sugar

1¼ cups self-rising white flour

1 teaspoon baking powder

½ teaspoon ground allspice

4 eggs

zest of 1 orange

1 tablespoon orange juice

½ cup ground almonds

1. Preheat the oven to 350°F. Grease the insides and line the bottoms of two 7-inch round cake pans (see page 212). Dust the pans with flour and shake out the excess (see page 213).

2. Cream the butter and sugar in a bowl until light and fluffy. Sift the flour, baking powder, and allspice onto the mixture, then fold it in. Add the eggs, orange zest and juice, and the ground almonds. Beat well. Stir in the grated carrots and chopped Brazil nuts.

¾ pound carrots,
peeled and finely
grated
I scant cup Brazil
nuts, coarsely
chopped and toasted

FOR THE FROSTING
I heaping cup
mascarpone or low-
fat cream cheese
I teaspoon finely
grated orange zest
(optional)
2 tablespoons orange
juice
2 tablespoons
powdered sugar

3. Divide the mixture evenly between the
two pans and level the surfaces. Bake for
35 to 40 minutes, or until risen and firm
to the touch. Transfer the pans to a wire
rack to cool.

4. For the frosting, beat together the
cheese, orange zest (if using), orange
juice, and powdered sugar in a bowl until
smooth.

5. Remove the cakes from the pans. To
assemble, transfer one cake to a serving
dish. Cover the surface of the cake with
half the frosting, then stack the second
cake on top. Spread the remainder of the
frosting onto the top of the cake, swirling
it attractively.

RASPBERRY AND PISTACHIO LAYER CAKE

THIS CAKE IS LIGHT, MOIST, AND EXCEPTIONALLY SPONGY. PISTACHIO NUTS FLAVOR THE CAKE, WHILE FRESH RASPBERRIES AND CREAM PROVIDE AN IRRESISTIBLE FILLING.

SERVES 8–10

½ cup shelled pistachio nuts

1¾ cups self-rising flour

2 teaspoons baking powder

4 eggs

1 cup + 2 tablespoons superfine sugar

2 sticks unsalted butter, softened

1 teaspoon vanilla extract

1. Preheat the oven to 325°F. Grease and line two 8-inch round cake pans (see page 212). Put the pistachio nuts in a bowl and cover with boiling water. Leave for 1 minute, then drain and remove the skins. Finely chop the nuts.

2. Sift the flour and baking powder into a bowl. Add the eggs, sugar, butter, and vanilla extract and beat, using an electric hand mixer, until pale and creamy. Stir in the chopped nuts.

3. Divide the batter evenly between the pans and level the surfaces. Bake for about 30 minutes, or until well risen and firm

FOR THE FILLING

5 tablespoons raspberry jam

⅔ cup heavy cream

1 cup raspberries

TO DECORATE

1¾ cups raspberries

¼ cup pistachio nuts

powdered sugar, for dusting (optional)

to the touch. Remove the cakes from the pans and transfer them to a wire rack to cool.

4. Heat the jam in a small pan until just melted. Set aside to cool. Place one cake on a serving plate. Whip the cream until peaks are just starting to form and spread it onto the cake. Scatter with the raspberries, then spoon the melted jam on top. Set the second cake on top.

5. To decorate, scatter the raspberries over the top of the cake. Skin the pistachios (following the instructions in step 1) and scatter them on top as well. Dust with powdered sugar, if desired. Keep in a cool place until ready to serve.

NOTE

THE MIXTURE SHOULD BE VERY SOFT AND DROP EASILY FROM A SPOON BEFORE BAKING. IF IT SEEMS A LITTLE STIFF, STIR IN A LITTLE MILK OR WATER.

Lovely Lemon Cake

This zesty lemon layer cake is perfect with a cup of coffee for an afternoon treat. The extra layer of lemon curd lifts it above and beyond a normal lemon drizzle cake.

SERVES 8–10

1¾ cups self-rising flour

4 eggs

1 cup + 2 tablespoons superfine sugar

2 sticks butter, softened

zest and juice of 1 lemon

½ cup lemon curd

FOR THE TOPPING

zest and juice of 1 lemon

¼ cup granulated sugar

1. Preheat the oven to 350°F. Grease the insides and line the bottoms of two 8-inch round cake pans (see page 212).

2. Sift the flour into a large bowl. Add the eggs, sugar, and butter. Beat, using an electric hand mixer, until pale and creamy.

3. Add the lemon zest and juice to the cake mixture, and mix well.

4. Divide the batter equally between the pans and level the surfaces. Bake for about 25 minutes, or until a knife inserted into the center comes out clean and the cakes are golden and have risen. Remove the cakes from the pans and transfer to a wire rack.

5. Once the cakes are cool, set one on a plate. Spread the lemon curd evenly onto it, then stack the second cake on top. Pierce the top layer all over with a skewer or toothpick.

6. To make the topping, mix the lemon zest with 1½ tablespoons of the sugar. Sprinkle the mixture onto the top layer of the cake.

7. In a small saucepan over low heat, simmer the lemon juice with the remaining sugar for a few minutes. Stir frequently, until you have a syrup. Drizzle evenly all over the top of the layer cake and serve.

RED VELVET CAKE

THIS CAKE IS SOMETHING OF A SHOWSTOPPER. THE FOUR DEEP-RED LAYERS OF SPONGE CAKE CONTRAST DRAMATICALLY WITH THE SNOWY WHITE CREAM-CHEESE FROSTING.

SERVES 12–14

3 cups all-purpose flour

¼ cup unsweetened cocoa powder

3 teaspoons baking powder

½ teaspoon baking soda

1¼ sticks unsalted butter

1½ cups superfine sugar

3 tablespoons + 1 teaspoon red food coloring

2 teaspoons vanilla extract

3 eggs

1. Preheat the oven to 350°F. Grease the insides and line the bottoms of four 8-inch round cake pans (see page 212). Sift together the flour, cocoa powder, baking powder, and baking soda a couple of times to make sure they are very well combined and aerated.

2. Beat together the butter and sugar until soft and fluffy, then add the food coloring and the vanilla extract. Beat again thoroughly.

3. Add the eggs one at a time, alternating with the flour mixture. Fold in the rest of the flour mixture, then mix in the buttermilk and the vinegar.

1 generous cup
buttermilk

1 teaspoon cider
vinegar

**FOR THE CREAM-
CHEESE FROSTING**

heaping ¾ cup regular
cream cheese

2¼ sticks unsalted
butter, softened

6 cups powdered
sugar, sifted

2 teaspoons vanilla
extract

TO DECORATE

red sprinkles

4. Divide the batter among the prepared cake pans and level the surfaces. Bake for about 30 minutes, or until well risen and firm to the touch. A skewer inserted in the center of the cake should come out clean.

5. For the frosting, beat together the cream cheese and butter until very soft and light, then gradually beat in the powdered sugar. This may feel quite stiff to start with, but keep beating and it will eventually soften and become extremely light and fluffy. Add the vanilla extract and beat for at least 5 minutes—this will ensure the frosting has sufficient volume to fill and cover the cake.

6. To assemble, stack the cakes, with some of the frosting between each layer, then cover the entire top and around the side. Decorate lavishly with red sprinkles.

A GREAT
EMPIRE, LIKE
A GREAT CAKE,
IS MOST EASILY
DIMINISHED AT
THE EDGES.

BENJAMIN
FRANKLIN

TO ASCERTAIN WHEN THEY ARE DONE, PLUNGE A CLEAN KNIFE INTO THE MIDDLE, AND IF ON WITHDRAWAL IT COMES OUT CLEAN, THE CAKES ARE DONE.

MRS. BEETON

BUTTERMILK
POUND CAKE

THE BEAUTY OF A POUND CAKE IS ITS SIMPLICITY, BECAUSE IT IS TRADITIONALLY MADE WITH EQUAL QUANTITIES OF ALL THE MAIN INGREDIENTS. HOWEVER, THIS VERSION HAS LESS BUTTER TO ALLOW FOR THE BUTTERMILK.

SERVES 8–10

1¾ cups self-rising flour

1¼ sticks unsalted butter

1 heaping cup superfine sugar, plus 2 tablespoons extra for sprinkling

3 eggs

scant ½ cup buttermilk

1 teaspoon vanilla extract

zest of 1 lemon

1. Preheat the oven to 350°F. Grease and line the bottom a deep 8-inch round cake pan or an 8 x 4 x 3-inch (6-cup) loaf pan (see page 212). Sift the flour twice to fully aerate it.

2. Beat the butter with an electric hand mixer until soft, then add the heaping cup of sugar. Continue to beat together until very light and fluffy. Mix in the eggs one at a time, alternating with tablespoons of the flour to stop the mixture from curdling. Fold in the rest of the flour with a large metal spoon. Stir in the buttermilk, vanilla extract, and lemon zest.

3. Add the batter to the prepared pan then sprinkle it evenly with the 2 tablespoons of sugar. Bake for about 50 minutes, or until golden brown and a skewer inserted in the center comes out clean. Let the cake cool in the pan for 10 minutes before removing it from the pan and transferring it to a wire rack to cool completely.

Vanilla Gugelhupf with Spiced Butter

Rich and sweet with a lovely moist texture, this delicious Austrian cake is similar to a brioche. It has a subtle flavoring of vanilla sugar, candied cherries, and citrus peel.

SERVES 10

9 tablespoons unsalted butter

2 cups all-purpose flour

a pinch of salt

2 teaspoons active dry yeast

3½ tablespoons superfine sugar

3½ tablespoons vanilla sugar (see page 217)

1 teaspoon vanilla extract

zest of 1 lemon

¼ cup chopped mixed candied peel

1. Melt the butter and let cool slightly. Sift the flour and salt into a bowl. Add the yeast, sugars, vanilla extract, lemon zest, peel, and cherries.

2. Add the milk and eggs to the melted butter, beat well, then add it to the flour mixture. Beat well for 2 minutes, then cover the bowl with plastic wrap and leave in a warm place until the mixture has doubled in size.

3. Meanwhile, make the spiced butter. Beat the ingredients in a bowl until thoroughly combined. Transfer to a small serving dish, cover loosely with plastic wrap, and keep in a cool place.

2 tablespoons candied
  red cherries, finely
  chopped

3 tablespoons milk

3 eggs

FOR THE SPICED
BUTTER

5 tablespoons unsalted
  butter, softened

1 tablespoon
  powdered sugar

¼ teaspoon ground
  nutmeg

½ teaspoon ground
  pumpkin pie spice

¼ teaspoon ground
  ginger

TO FINISH

powdered sugar, for
  dusting

4. Brush the inside of a 7-cup Bundt pan
with a little melted butter. Dust with flour
and shake out the excess (see page 213).

5. Lightly beat the risen dough to reduce
the volume, then add it to the prepared
pan. Cover with oiled plastic wrap and let
rise until the dough almost reaches the top
of the pan.

6. Preheat the oven to 400°F. Bake for
25 to 30 minutes, or until deep golden in
color. Leave in the pan for 5 minutes, then
loosen the edges with a knife. Invert the
pan onto a wire rack and tap the pan to
help ease the cake out. Let cool slightly
before serving, dusted with powdered
sugar and accompanied by the spiced
butter.

NOTE

EVEN THOUGH THIS
CAKE IS VERY EASY
TO MAKE, ALLOW
PLENTY OF TIME FOR
THE DOUGH TO RISE.
THIS MIGHT TAKE
2 HOURS FOR THE
FIRST PROVING AND
A FURTHER HOUR
IN THE PAN.

Coffee Marsala Cake with Marsala Cream

THIS IS A VERY GROWN-UP CAKE, REMINISCENT OF A BOOZY TIRAMISU. THE ADDITION OF COFFEE STOPS IT FROM BEING OVERLY SWEET.

SERVES 8–10

1 ¾ cups self-rising flour

1 tablespoon instant espresso granules

2 sticks unsalted butter

1 ¼ cups soft light brown sugar

4 eggs

1 tablespoon Marsala wine

1 teaspoon vanilla extract

3 tablespoons milk

1. Preheat the oven to 350°F. Grease and line two deep 8-inch round cake pans (see page 212). Sift the flour and espresso granules together.

2. Beat the butter with an electric hand mixer until soft, then add the sugar. Continue to beat until light and fluffy. Beat in the eggs one at a time, alternating with tablespoons of the flour mixture to stop it from curdling. Gently fold in the remaining flour, then stir in all of the liquid ingredients. You should have a soft, dropping consistency.

FOR THE MARSALA CREAM

½ teaspoon instant espresso granules

1¼ cups heavy cream

2 tablespoons Marsala wine

1 tablespoon powdered sugar

3. Divide the batter between the prepared cake pans and level the surfaces. Bake for about 25 minutes, or until well risen and firm to the touch. Let the cakes cool in their pans for 10 minutes, then remove them from the pans and transfer them to a wire rack to cool.

4. To make the Marsala cream, dissolve the espresso granules in 1 tablespoon of boiling water. Whip the cream until thick and fairly stiff, then fold in the espresso, Marsala wine, and the powdered sugar. Mix together thoroughly but lightly.

5. To assemble, place one cake on a serving plate and spread one-third of the cream onto it. Stack the other cake on top. Cover the top and around the sides with the remaining cream.

NOTE

DON'T BE TEMPTED TO SUBSTITUTE THE ESPRESSO GRANULES WITH REGULAR INSTANT COFFEE GRANULES.

TRANQUIL
TARTS

TREACLE TART

THIS ROBUST PUDDING ILLUSTRATES HOW THE SIMPLEST INGREDIENTS CAN BE TRANSFORMED INTO A MOST HEAVENLY DESSERT.

SERVES 8–10

1¾ cups all-purpose flour

1¼ sticks unsalted butter, chilled

1 egg yolk

1 tablespoon superfine sugar

FOR THE FILLING

2 cups light corn syrup

1¾ cups white breadcrumbs

zest of 3 lemons

2 eggs

TO SERVE

vanilla ice cream or crème fraîche

1. To make the pastry, sift the flour and put it in a food processor. Cut the butter into small pieces, add it to the flour, and process until the mixture resembles breadcrumbs. Add the egg yolk, sugar, and about 2 tablespoons of cold water. Process briefly to a firm dough. Turn out onto a lightly floured surface and knead lightly, then seal in plastic wrap and chill in the fridge for 30 minutes.

2. Preheat the oven to 350°F. Roll out the pastry on a lightly floured surface and use it to line a 9½-inch round fluted French tart pan, with sides about 1½ inches deep (see page 215). Trim off the excess pastry and flute the edges. Pierce the dough on the bottom of the pan all over with a fork.

3. For the filling, gently warm the light corn syrup in a saucepan over low heat. When it has thinned in consistency remove from the heat and mix it with the breadcrumbs and lemon zest. Lightly beat the eggs and stir them into the syrup mixture to combine. Pour the filling into the pastry shell and smooth the surface.

4. Bake for 45 to 50 minutes, or until the filling is lightly set and turning golden. Let cool slightly. Serve warm, with vanilla ice cream or crème fraîche.

TIRAMISU TORTE

AN OUTRAGEOUSLY RICH DESSERT WITH AN IRRESISTIBLY GOOEY
TEXTURE. A CREAMY RUM AND VANILLA MIXTURE IS MARBLED
INTO DARK CHOCOLATE, COFFEE, AND LIQUEUR, POURED INTO AN
AMARETTI COOKIE PASTRY SHELL, AND BAKED.

SERVES 8–10

10 ounces amaretti
cookies

9 tablespoons
unsalted butter

FOR THE FILLING

3¼ cups mascarpone
cheese or 2¾
cups regular cream
cheese (at room
temperature)

⅔ cup superfine sugar

3 eggs, separated

¼ cup all-purpose
flour

3 tablespoons dark
rum

1. Place the cookies in a blender or food
processor and process until finely ground.
Melt 5 tablespoons of the butter, place in
a bowl, and stir in the crumbs to combine.
Spoon into a 9-inch round springform
pan. Press evenly over the bottom and 1½
inches up the inside, using the back of a
spoon to form a neat pastry shell. Chill for
at least 30 minutes, or until firm.

2. Preheat the oven to 400°F. Using a
wooden spoon, beat the mascarpone or
cream cheese until smooth. Add the sugar
and beat again until very smooth, then beat
in the egg yolks. Divide the mixture in half
and stir the flour, rum, and vanilla extract
into one half.

½ teaspoon vanilla
extract

6 ounces baking
chocolate (at least
70% cocoa solids)

1 tablespoon instant
espresso granules

3 tablespoons Tia
Maria or other
coffee liqueur

TO FINISH

powdered sugar, for
dusting (optional)

TO SERVE

crème fraîche or
sour cream

3. Break up the chocolate and add it to a heatproof bowl set over a pan of simmering water (see page 218). After it has melted let it cool slightly, then stir in the espresso granules and liqueur. Stir into the remaining half of the soft cheese mixture. Beat the egg whites until just holding soft peaks and fold half into each flavored cheese mixture.

4. Quickly spoon alternating mounds of the two cheese mixtures into the pastry shell to fill. Using a metal spatula, swirl the mixtures together to produce a marbled effect.

5. Bake for 45 minutes, covering the top with foil if it appears to be browning too quickly. At this stage the torte will be soft in the middle. Leave it in the turned-off oven with the door slightly ajar to cool completely; it will continue to firm up during this time. Chill for several hours before serving, to allow the flavors to develop.

6. If desired, dust the top of the torte with powdered sugar. Slice into wedges, and serve with a little crème fraîche or sour cream on the side.

PART OF
THE SECRET OF
SUCCESS IN LIFE IS
TO EAT WHAT YOU
LIKE AND LET THE
FOOD FIGHT IT
OUT INSIDE.

MARK TWAIN

TARTE TATIN

THIS CLASSIC FRENCH DESSERT IS COOKED UPSIDE DOWN. AFTER
BAKING, THE TART IS TURNED OVER SO THE FRUIT LAYER IS ON TOP
AND THE BUTTERY, CARAMEL JUICES OOZE INTO THE PASTRY.

SERVES 6

8 ounces ready-made
  puff pastry (or ⅓ of
  the recipe on page
  214)

FOR THE FILLING

heaping ⅓ cup
  superfine sugar
4–5 apples
3½ tablespoons
  unsalted butter,
  cubed

TO SERVE

vanilla ice cream

1. First make the filling. Put the sugar
in a saucepan over low heat and add 3
tablespoons of water. Stir occasionally
until the sugar dissolves, then increase
the heat and, without stirring, cook the
syrup to a rich caramel. Carefully pour it
into a shallow, heavy 8-inch cake pan or
an ovenproof skillet and swirl it around to
coat the bottom evenly.

2. Preheat the oven to 425°F. Cut the
apples in half, peel them, and then scoop
out the cores with a teaspoon.

3. Scatter the caramel with half of the
butter cubes. Arrange the apple halves,
curved-side down, on top. Pack them in
as tightly as possible. Fill any gaps with

smaller wedges of apple. Scatter the remaining butter cubes on top. Place the pan or skillet over medium heat and cook for about 5 minutes to partly cook and lightly brown the apples. Watch carefully to ensure the apples do not burn.

4. Roll out the puff pastry on a lightly floured surface to form a round disk slightly larger than the diameter of the pan or skillet. Pierce the pastry all over with a fork. Carefully lift the pastry and place it on top of the apples. Pat it gently, tucking the edges of the pastry down the inside of the sides of the pan or skillet. Bake for 20 to 25 minutes, or until the pastry is well risen, crisp, and golden brown.

5. Let cool for 10 minutes. To remove the tart from the pan, cover it with a large inverted serving plate. Carefully tip out any cooking juices into a bowl. Then, holding the pan and plate tightly together, quickly turn the pan and plate over all at once so the plate is the right way up. Give the base of the pan a few sharp taps, then carefully lift it off of the tart. Drizzle the buttery juices onto the tart and serve immediately, cut into wedges, with a dollop or two of vanilla ice cream.

**CUSTARD:
A DETESTABLE
SUBSTANCE
PRODUCED BY
A MALEVOLENT
CONSPIRACY OF
THE HEN, THE COW,
AND THE COOK.**

AMBROSE
BIERCE

RASPBERRY AND VANILLA CUSTARD TART

IN THIS SUMMERY TART, SWEET RASPBERRIES, COVERED WITH A LIBERAL
DUSTING OF VANILLA SUGAR, PERCH ON A CREAMY VANILLA CUSTARD.

SERVES 6

1¼ cups all-purpose
  flour

9 tablespoons
  unsalted butter,
  chilled and diced

2 tablespoons
  vanilla sugar
  (see page 217)

1 teaspoon finely
  grated orange zest

1 egg yolk

1. To make the pastry, sift the flour
into a bowl. Rub in the butter, using your
fingertips. Add the vanilla sugar and orange
zest. Then, using a round-bladed knife, mix
in the egg yolk, along with 2 to 3 teaspoons
of cold water to form a stiff dough.

2. Knead the pastry dough briefly until
smooth. Seal in plastic wrap and chill in the
fridge for 20 minutes.

3. Preheat the oven to 400°F. Butter an
8-inch round fluted French tart pan with a
removable bottom.

4. Roll out the dough on a lightly floured
work surface then use it to line the
prepared pan (see page 215). Chill again

FOR THE VANILLA CUSTARD

2 eggs

2 egg yolks

3½ tablespoons superfine sugar

½ vanilla bean

scant 2 cups light cream

TO FINISH

1¼ cups raspberries

vanilla sugar, for dusting

NOTE

DO NOT OVERCOOK THE CUSTARD FILLING: IT SHOULD STILL WOBBLE SLIGHTLY IN THE CENTER WHEN IT IS DONE.

for 20 minutes. Line the pastry shell with wax paper or foil. Add baking beans and bake blind (see page 215) for 15 minutes. Remove the baking beans and paper or foil and return the pan to the oven for 5 to 10 minutes to cook the bottom of the pastry shell.

5. To make the custard filling, beat the whole eggs, egg yolks, and sugar in a bowl. Split the vanilla bean, scrape out the seeds, and place the bean and seeds in a small pan with the cream. Cook over very low heat until the cream is well flavored and almost boiling. Add the hot cream to the egg mixture, whisking constantly, then strain into the pastry shell.

6. Lower the oven temperature to 300°F. Place the tart in the oven and bake for 45 minutes, or until the center is lightly set. Remove from the oven and set aside until completely cool.

7. Carefully remove the tart from the pan. To finish, arrange the raspberries on top of the vanilla custard and dust liberally with vanilla sugar to serve.

WALNUT TART WITH CARAMEL ICE CREAM

WALNUTS AND CARAMEL ARE A MARRIAGE MADE IN HEAVEN. IN THIS DELIGHTFULLY DELICIOUS TART THE WALNUTS ARE ENCASED IN AN IRRESISTIBLE GOOEY FUDGE MIXTURE.

SERVES 8–10

1¾ cups all-purpose flour

2 tablespoons powdered sugar

9 tablespoons unsalted butter, chilled and diced

2 egg yolks

FOR THE FILLING

9 tablespoons unsalted butter, softened

⅔ cup light brown sugar

3 eggs

1. First make the ice cream. Put the sugar in a saucepan with ⅔ cup of the water. Dissolve over low heat until clear. Increase the heat and boil rapidly until the sugar begins to caramelize.

2. Remove from the heat and let the caramel stand for 2 to 3 minutes; it will turn a deep amber-brown color. Stir in the milk and cream, then beat in the egg yolks. Return to low heat and stir, without letting the custard boil, for about 15 minutes, or until slightly thickened. Remove from the heat, let cool, then chill in the fridge.

3. Freeze the ice cream, using an ice-cream machine if you have one.

finely grated zest
and juice of
1 small orange
½ cup golden syrup
1¾ cups walnut
pieces
a pinch of salt

**FOR THE CARAMEL
ICE CREAM**
heaping ¾ cup
granulated sugar
1¼ cups milk
1¼ cups heavy cream
8 egg yolks

Alternatively, pour the mixture into a freezerproof container and freeze until firm.

4. To make the pastry, sift the flour and powdered sugar together into a bowl and rub in the diced butter. Stir in the egg yolks and enough ice-cold water to bind the mixture to a firm dough. Knead lightly until smooth. Seal in plastic wrap and chill for 30 minutes.

5. Preheat the oven to 400°F. Roll the pastry out thinly and use it to line a 9½-inch round fluted French tart pan with a removable bottom (see page 215). Chill the pastry for 20 minutes. Line with wax paper, add baking beans, and bake blind (see page 215) for 15 to 20 minutes, removing the paper and beans for the last 5 minutes. Lower the oven temperature to 350°F.

6. To make the filling, cream the butter and sugar together until light and fluffy. Gradually beat in the eggs, one at a time, then stir in the orange zest and juice.

Heat the syrup until runny but not very hot, then stir it into the filling with the walnuts and salt. Pour the mixture into the pastry shell and bake for 40 to 45 minutes, or until lightly browned and risen. (The tart will sink a little as it cools.) Serve warm or cold with a scoop of the caramel ice cream on the side.

LIFE IS UNCERTAIN. EAT DESSERT FIRST.

ERNESTINE ULMER

BAKEWELL TART

THIS RECIPE RESTORES ONE OF BRITAIN'S MOST FAMOUS DESSERTS TO ITS ORIGINAL GLORY. HERE, A DEEP ALMOND SPONGE CAKE AND THICK APRICOT CONSERVE ARE ENCLOSED IN A PASTRY SHELL.

SERVES 8

1¾ cups all-purpose flour

¼ cup lightly salted butter

¼ cup vegetable shortening

FOR THE FILLING

¼ cup apricot conserve or jam

2 ounces amaretti cookies

5 tablespoons unsalted butter

3 eggs

½ cup + 2 tablespoons superfine sugar

1. To make the pastry, sift the flour into a bowl. Dice the butter and shortening into small pieces, and rub the dice into the flour using your fingertips. Stir in enough cold water to make a firm dough. Knead lightly, then seal the dough in plastic wrap and let chill for 30 minutes.

2. Preheat the oven to 400°F and set a baking pan in the oven. Roll out the pastry on a lightly floured surface and use it to line a 9-inch round springform pan (see page 212). Spread the apricot conserve evenly over the bottom of the pastry. Halve the amaretti cookies and set aside.

1 teaspoon almond
   extract
1¼ cups ground
   almonds

TO SERVE
caramel oranges
   (see page 202),
   optional
1 tablespoon
   powdered sugar,
   for dusting
cream or crème
   fraîche

3. Melt the butter and set aside. Put the eggs and sugar in a large bowl and beat until the mixture is thick enough to leave a trail on the surface when the beater is lifted away. Pour the melted butter in around the edge of the bowl. Add the almond extract, then scatter the ground almonds and amaretti cookies on top. Using a large metal spoon, gently fold everything into the mixture until just combined.

4. Pour the mixture into the pastry shell. Place on the preheated baking pan and bake for 10 minutes. Lower the oven temperature to 350°F and bake for 40 minutes longer, or until the filling is firm and set.

5. If serving with the caramel oranges, arrange some on top of the tart, spooning a little of the syrup onto them. Let the tart cool slightly, then remove from the pan and transfer to a serving plate. Dust with powdered sugar and serve with cream or crème fraîche and the rest of the oranges.

3 oranges

¾ cup + 2 tablespoons superfine sugar

CARAMEL ORANGES

Peel strips of zest off of one of the oranges and reserve. Then peel all 3 oranges, discarding all the white pith. Slice the peeled oranges thinly. Dissolve the sugar in 2½ cups of water in a heavy pan over low heat. Increase the heat and boil steadily for 5 minutes. Add the reserved orange zest and orange slices. Bring to a boil, then simmer gently for 15 minutes. Remove the zest and fruit with a slotted spoon and cook the syrup for 20 minutes longer, or until pale golden. Return the fruit to the syrup. Let cool a little before serving.

NOTE

DON'T WORRY IF THE TART SINKS SLIGHTLY IN THE CENTER. THIS WILL ACCENTUATE ITS LOVELY CRACKED PASTRY SHELL.

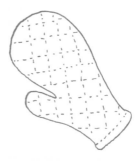

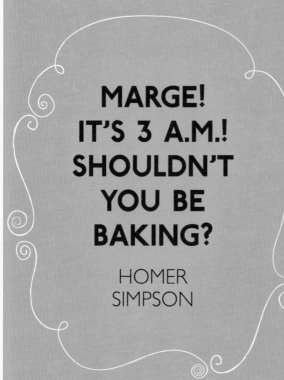

WALNUT AND ORANGE TORTE

FOLDING WHISKED EGG WHITES INTO THE CREAMED MIXTURE GIVES A SOUFFLÉ QUALITY TO THIS AIRY SPONGE CAKE.

SERVES 8–10

1½ cups walnut halves

1¼ sticks unsalted butter, softened

¾ cup superfine sugar

5 eggs, separated

zest of 1 orange

⅔ cup ricotta cheese

⅓ cup all-purpose flour

1. Preheat the oven to 375°F. Grease and line a 9-inch round springform pan (see page 212). Lightly toast the walnuts, let cool, then chop roughly. Set aside ¼ cup for the decoration.

2. Cream the butter and ½ cup plus 2 tablespoons of the sugar together in a bowl until light and fluffy. Add the egg yolks, orange zest, ricotta cheese, flour, and roughly chopped walnuts. Mix gently to combine.

3. Put the egg whites into a large bowl and beat until stiff but not dry. Gradually beat in the remaining sugar. Using a large metal spoon, fold one-quarter of the

TO FINISH

⅓ cup apricot jam

2 teaspoons orange juice

1 ounce baking chocolate (at least 70% cocoa solids), in one piece (at room temperature)

egg-white mixture into the cheese mixture to loosen it slightly, then carefully fold in the rest of the egg-white mixture to combine.

4. Pour the batter into the prepared pan and gently level the surface. Bake for about 30 minutes, or until risen and just firm to the touch. Remove from the oven and leave to cool in the pan.

5. Heat the apricot jam in a pan until melted, then press through a strainer into a bowl. Stir in the orange juice to make a glaze.

6. Brush half of the apricot glaze around the side of the cake. Using a metal spatula, coat the side of the cake with the reserved chopped walnuts.

7. Brush the remaining apricot glaze onto the top of the cake. Using a vegetable peeler, shave simple curls from the chocolate (or, for long, thin curls, see page 219). Scatter the top of the cake with the chocolate curls and serve in slices.

VARIATION

OMIT THE CHOCOLATE CURLS. COVER THE TOP OF THE CAKE WITH HALVED AND PITTED SMALL PLUMS. GLAZE THE FRUIT WITH ¼ CUP OF WARMED AND STRAINED PLUM JAM.

Rum, Raisin, and White Chocolate Tart

This delicious tart has a layer of rum-soaked raisins hidden beneath a chewy almond topping, which is heavily speckled with chunky pieces of white chocolate.

SERVES 8

1½ cups raisins

generous ⅓ cup rum

1¼ cups all-purpose flour

a pinch of salt

5 tablespoons unsalted butter, diced

heaping ⅓ cup superfine sugar

3 egg yolks

1. Add the raisins to a bowl and pour in the rum. Let stand until the raisins have absorbed most of the rum.

2. To make the pastry, sift the flour and salt into a large bowl. Rub in the diced butter until the mixture resembles breadcrumbs. Stir in the sugar and yolks. Mix them to a smooth dough (add 1 teaspoon of cold water if necessary to bind the dough together). Knead lightly, seal in plastic wrap, and chill for 30 minutes.

3. Preheat the oven to 375°F. Roll out the pastry on a lightly floured work surface and use it to line a 9½-inch round French

FOR THE FILLING

3 tablespoons raw almonds

¾ pound white chocolate

3½ tablespoons unsalted butter

⅔ cup light brown sugar

2 eggs

1 cup self-rising flour

TO FINISH

1 tablespoon powdered sugar, for dusting

tart pan with a removable bottom (see page 215).

Line the pastry shell with wax paper and fill it with baking beans. Bake blind (see page 215) for 15 minutes, then remove the paper and beans and bake for 5 minutes longer, then let it cool. Lower the oven temperature to 350°F.

4. Spoon the raisins and any rum into the pastry shell. For the filling, roughly chop the almonds. Chop 10½ ounces of the white chocolate into small pieces.

5. Break up the remaining chocolate and add it to a heatproof bowl set over a pan of barely simmering water (see page 218). Add the butter and let melt.

6. Beat the sugar and eggs together in a bowl. Stir in the flour, melted chocolate, and three-quarters of the chopped chocolate. Pour the batter into the pastry shell. Scatter with the remaining chocolate and the almonds and bake for 40 minutes, or until just firm. Cover the tart with foil about halfway through cooking to stop it from overbrowning. Serve warm, dusted with powdered sugar.

NOTE

IF YOU HAVE TIME, SOAK THE RAISINS IN THE RUM OVERNIGHT TO ALLOW THEM TO PLUMP UP THOROUGHLY.

MINCEMEAT FLAN

THE MINCEMEAT NEEDS TO BE PREPARED AT LEAST 2 WEEKS IN
ADVANCE TO ALLOW IT TO MATURE.

SERVES 10

⅓ cup blanched
  almonds
1 cup all-purpose
  flour
a pinch of salt
zest and juice of
  1 orange
¼ cup superfine sugar
3½ tablespoons
  unsalted butter,
  diced
1 egg yolk
3 medium bananas
2 teaspoons lemon
  juice
3 ripe star fruit
honey, for brushing

1. To make the mincemeat, core and
grate the apple, then roughly chop the
cherries and almonds. Blend the currants
and raisins in a food processor for 30
seconds, then stir into the apple mixture,
together with the remaining ingredients.
Mix well. Cover and let macerate for 2
days in a cool place. Pack into sterilized
jars and seal.

2. For the pastry, toast the almonds until
evenly golden. Let them cool, then grind
finely in a food processor.

3. Sift the flour and salt into a bowl
and stir in the almonds, orange zest, and
sugar. Rub in the butter until the mixture
resembles breadcrumbs. Beat the egg yolk
with 2 tablespoons of orange juice and
stir into the mixture until it begins to hold

FOR THE MINCEMEAT

1 large cooking apple

3½ tablespoons candied red cherries

⅓ cup blanched almonds

1¾ cups currants

1¾ cups golden raisins

⅔ cup chopped candied peel

1¼ cups soft dark brown sugar

4½ ounces shredded suet

1 teaspoon ground cinnamon

½ teaspoon grated nutmeg

zest and juice of 1 orange

⅔ cup brandy or rum

NOTE

THE BASIC MINCEMEAT RECIPE MAKES ABOUT 3 POUNDS, WHICH IS MORE THAN YOU WILL NEED FOR THIS FLAN. USE THE REST TO MAKE INDIVIDUAL MINCE TARTLETS.

together, adding more juice if necessary. Knead the dough lightly on a clean work surface until smooth. Wrap and chill for at least 1 hour. This pastry is very crumbly.

4. Allow the pastry to come to room temperature. Peel and cube the bananas, then toss the cubes in the lemon juice. Mix the cubes with two-thirds of the mincemeat, then set aside.

5. Roll out the pastry and use it to line a 9½-inch round French tart pan (see page 215). Chill for 15 minutes.

6. Preheat the oven to 375°F. Spoon the mincemeat and banana mixture evenly into the tart pan. Bake for 35 to 40 minutes, or until the pastry is golden brown.

7. Meanwhile, preheat the broiler to high. Cut the star fruit into ¼-inch slices and place on a foil-lined broiler pan. Brush with a little warmed honey and broil for 3 to 5 minutes, watching them closely. Remove from the heat and let cool.

8. Decorate the flan with the star fruit and serve warm.

STEP-BY-STEP
TECHNIQUES

Preparing Pans

To make most cakes you need to line the pans with wax paper or nonstick parchment paper first. The latter is used for cakes that are more likely to stick, such as roulades (roll cakes) and meringues.

Round

Place the pan on a piece of wax paper or nonstick parchment paper and draw around it. Cut out the circle, just inside the line. Now, cut strip(s) of paper, about ¾ inch wider than the depth of the pan. Fold up the bottom edge by ½ inch, then make cuts, 1 inch apart, from edge to fold, all the way around. Grease the pan. Position the paper strip(s) around the side of the pan so that the snipped edge sits on the bottom. Set the paper circle into the bottom, then grease all of the paper.

Square or Rectangular

Cut a piece of wax paper or nonstick parchment paper fractionally smaller than the base of the pan. For the sides, cut strips about ¾ inch wider than the depth of the pan. Fold up the bottom edge by ¼ inch. Grease the pan. Make a cut from the edge of the paper to the fold and press into one corner. Continue fitting the paper around the pan, cutting it to fit at each corner. Place the piece of paper in the bottom, then grease all of the paper.

Loaf

Grease the bottom and inside of the loaf pan. Cut a strip of wax paper or nonstick parchment paper the length of the pan base and wide enough to cover the bottom and long sides. Press into position in the pan. Cut another strip the width of the pan base and long enough to cover the bottom and ends of the pan. Press into position. Grease all of the paper. Sometimes only the bottom and the long sides of a loaf pan need to be lined. In this case, use a double thickness of paper so you can lift the loaf from the pan easily after baking.

Jelly roll

Grease the bottom and inside of the pan. Cut a rectangle of wax paper or nonstick parchment paper about 3 inches wider and longer than the size of the pan. Press the paper into the pan, cutting the paper at the corners and folding it to fit neatly. Grease the paper.

Layer cake

Place the round cake pan on a piece of wax paper or nonstick parchment paper and draw around it. Cut out, just inside the line. Grease the bottom and inside of the pan and set the paper into the bottom. Grease the paper. Sprinkle a little flour into the pan. Tap and tilt the pan until the flour coats the bottom and the inside walls, leaving no bare spots. Tip out and discard any excess flour.

Puff Pastry

This is the richest of all pastries. Ready-made puff pastry is widely available, both fresh and frozen. To make it requires patience, practice, and very light handling. Whenever possible it should be made the day before use. It is not practical to make in a quantity using less than 3¾ cups flour, but it can be frozen. The quantity given here yields the same as two 13-ounce packages of ready-made puff pastry.

> **3¾ CUPS BREAD FLOUR**
> **A PINCH OF SALT**
> **4 STICKS UNSALTED BUTTER, CHILLED**
> **1 TABLESPOON LEMON JUICE**

1. Mix the flour and salt together in a bowl. Slice off 3½ tablespoons of the butter and cut into dice. Flatten the remaining butter with a rolling pin to form a slab ¾ inch thick.

2. Rub the diced butter into the flour using your fingertips. Using a round-bladed knife or metal spatula, stir in the lemon juice and about 1¼ cups chilled water or enough to make a soft dough.

3. Quickly knead the dough until smooth and shape into a disk. Cut through half the depth in the shape of a cross. Open out to form a star.

4. Roll out, keeping the center four times as thick as the flaps. Place the slab of butter in the center.

5. Fold the flaps envelope-style gently with a rolling pin. Roll out to a 16 x 8-inch rectangle.

6. Fold the bottom third up away from you, and the top third down, toward you, keeping the edges straight. Seal the edges. Seal in plastic wrap and leave to rest in the fridge for 30 minutes.

7. Place the pastry on a lightly floured surface with the folded edges to the sides, then repeat the rolling, folding, and resting sequence five times.

Lining a French Tart Pan

A French tart pan with a removable bottom is ideal because it transfers heat rapidly and the pastry tends to cook better than in a china or ceramic dish. The removable bottom also makes it easier to transfer the baked tart or flan to a serving plate.

1. Roll out the pastry on a lightly floured surface until it is about 2 inches larger than the French tart pan all the way around. Use the rolling pin to help you lift the pastry over the pan.

2. Lift the edges of the pastry so that it drops down into the pan, then gently press the pastry against the edges of the pan so that there are no gaps between the pastry and the pan.

3. Turn any surplus pastry outward over the rim of the pan and trim the pastry edges with a sharp knife to neaten. Alternatively, you can roll the rolling pin over the top of the pan to cut off excess pastry.

Baking Blind

If a recipe instructs you to bake blind, it means that you should bake the pastry shell (or shells) before adding any filling. The pastry may be partially baked before adding the filling, or it may be completely baked if the filling doesn't require further cooking. Fully baked pastry shells keep for several days sealed in plastic wrap or can be frozen.

1. Line the flan or tart pan or dish with pastry (see above). If you have time, chill the pastry shell in the fridge for 20 to 30 minutes to rest the pastry and help reduce shrinkage during baking. Pierce the bottom of the pastry shell evenly with a fork, then line with a piece of wax paper or foil that is larger than the pastry shell.

2. Fill with ceramic baking beans or dried legumes and spread them evenly all over the unbaked pastry. (Individual tartlet pastry shells don't need lining; it should be sufficient to prick them with a fork.)

3. For partially baked cases, bake at 400°F for 10 to 15 minutes, or until the shell looks "set." Carefully remove the paper or foil and the beans and bake for 5 minutes more, until the bottom is firm to the touch and lightly colored. Pastry shells that require complete baking should be returned to the oven for about 15 minutes, or until firm and golden brown.

MAKING CUSTARD

This is a recipe for making "real" custard. It can also form the basis of several creamy desserts.

3 EGG YOLKS
2 TABLESPOONS SUPERFINE SUGAR
½ TEASPOON CORNSTARCH
1¼ CUPS MILK
½ TEASPOON VANILLA EXTRACT

NOTE

A TRADITIONAL EGG CUSTARD DOESN'T INCLUDE CORNSTARCH, BUT YOU WILL FIND THAT INCORPORATING A LITTLE GREATLY REDUCES THE RISK OF CURDLING.

1. Place the egg yolks, sugar, and cornstarch in a bowl with a little of the milk and beat until smooth.

2. 2. Bring the remaining milk to a boil in a heavy saucepan. Add the milk to the egg-yolk mixture, beating well. Return to the saucepan and add the vanilla extract.

3. 3. Cook over the lowest possible heat, stirring constantly, for about 10 minutes, or until the custard thickens slightly. It should be thick enough to thinly coat the back of a wooden spoon. Do not boil; otherwise, the custard may curdle. Strain and serve.

Vanilla Sugar

To make your own vanilla sugar, simply bury a vanilla bean in a jar of superfine sugar and leave it for a couple of days before using the sugar. The sugar level can be replenished as you use it.

If you don't have any vanilla sugar on hand when you need it, you can use ordinary superfine sugar and a generous splash of vanilla extract as a substitute.

Covering a Cake with Marzipan

1. Trim the top of the cake so that it is flat and level. Turn the cake over so that the flat bottom becomes the top. Place on a cake board, which should be at least 2 inches larger than the cake, and set aside.

2. On a work surface dusted with powdered sugar, roll out half of the marzipan to fit the top of the cake and set it aside. Brush the top of the cake with apricot glaze (melted jam).

3. Lift the marzipan onto the top of the cake and smooth it over, neatening the edges.

4. Cut a piece of string the same height as the cake with its marzipan top, and another to fit around the circumference of the cake. Roll out the remaining marzipan and, using the string as a guide, trim it to size. Brush the side of the cake and the top rim of the marzipan with apricot glaze.

5. Loosely roll up the marzipan strip. Place one end against the side of the cake, then unroll it to cover the cake all the way around. Use a metal spatula to smooth it over, and blend the line where it meets.

6. Flatten the top lightly with a rolling pin. Leave the cake in a cool, dry room to dry out thoroughly for about 2 days before applying frosting, royal icing, or gum paste.

Applying Gum Paste

1. Dust your work surface and rolling pin with cornstarch. Knead the gum paste until pliable. Roll out into a round or square that is 2 to 3 inches larger than the cake all the way around.

2. With the help of a rolling pin, lift the gum paste over the top of the cake and allow it to drape over the edges of the cake. Dust your hands with cornstarch and press the gum paste onto the top and around the side of the cake, easing it down to the cake board or plate.

3. Trim off any excess gum paste at the bottom edge.

4. Dust your fingers with a little cornstarch, then gently rub the gum paste in a circular movement to buff and smooth the surface.

Melting Chocolate

On the Stove

Break the chocolate into pieces and place in a heatproof bowl. Set the bowl over a pan of barely simmering water and leave until melted (make sure the base of the bowl doesn't touch the simmering water). Once melted, gently stir the chocolate until completely smooth. Remove the bowl from the pan, ensuring that any water droplets on the bowl do not come into contact with the chocolate.

In the Microwave

Break the chocolate into pieces and place in a small heatproof bowl. The time will vary according to the initial temperature of the chocolate, the amount used, and the type of bowl. As a guide, microwave baking chocolate or milk chocolate on high, allowing about 2 minutes for 4½ ounces of chocolate and 3 minutes for 6 to 8 ounces. Because it is more likely to overheat, white chocolate is best melted on medium.

Chocolate Curls

Spread melted chocolate on a marble slab or clean work surface and let set until no longer sticky to the touch. Holding a large knife at a slight angle to the surface, push the blade across the chocolate to shave off long, thin curls. Adjust the angle of the blade to obtain the best curls. If the chocolate breaks into brittle pieces, then it has become too cold and should be left to soften before trying again.

For simple chocolate curls, use a large chunky bar of chocolate at room temperature and shave off curls using a vegetable peeler.

Dipped Fruits and Nuts

Choose small, whole fruits that are ripe but not soft. Strawberries, cherries, grapes, kumquats, and gooseberries are ideal. (Brazil nuts and pecans work well, too.) Wash the fruit if necessary and dry thoroughly.

1. Melt a little chocolate in a small bowl (see previous page). Half-dip the fruit and/or nuts in the chocolate, letting the excess chocolate drip back into the bowl.

2. Place the dipped fruits on a sheet of wax paper to set.

INDEX

LET
THEM EAT
CAKE.

MARIE
ANTOINETTE